THE FIRST
PAUL

THE FIRST PAUL

Reclaiming the Radical Visionary
Behind the Church's Conservative Icon

MARCUS J. BORG

JOHN DOMINIC CROSSAN

HarperOne
An Imprint of HarperCollinsPublishers

HarperOne

THE FIRST PAUL: *Reclaiming the Radical Visionary Behind the Church's Conservative Icon.* Copyright © 2009 by Marcus J. Borg and John Dominic Crossan. All rights reserved. Printed in the United States of America. No part of this book may be used or reproduced in any manner whatsoever without written permission except in the case of brief quotations embodied in critical articles and reviews. For information address HarperCollins Publishers, 195 Broadway, New York, NY 10007.

HarperCollins books may be purchased for educational, business, or sales promotional use. For information, please e-mail the Special Markets Department at SPsales@harpercollins.com.

HarperCollins Web site: http://www.harpercollins.com

HarperCollins®, ■®, and HarperOne™ are trademarks of HarperCollins Publishers.

FIRST HARPERCOLLINS PAPERBACK EDITION PUBLISHED IN 2010

Library of Congress Cataloging-in-Publication Data is available upon request.

ISBN 978–0–06–143073–2

17 18 19 RRD(C) 10 9 8

CONTENTS

THE FIRST
PAUL

CHAPTER ONE

PAUL: APPEALING OR APPALLING?

PAUL IS SECOND ONLY TO JESUS as the most important person in the origins of Christianity. Yet he is not universally well regarded, even among Christians. Some find him appealing, and others find him appalling; some aren't sure what to think of him, and others know little about him.

The cover of *Newsweek* for May 6, 2002, asked, "What Would Jesus Do?" The story inside referred to Paul as well, citing passages attributed to him on slavery, anti-Semitism, misogyny, and heterosexism:

> The Biblical defense of slavery is: "Slaves, obey your earthly masters with fear and trembling, in singleness of heart as you obey Christ," writes Saint Paul. Anti-Semitism was long justified by passages like this one from I Thessalonians: the Jews "killed both the Lord Jesus and the prophets." And the subjugation of women had

a foundation in I Timothy: "As in all the churches of the saints, women should be silent in the churches. . . . If there is anything they desire to know, let them ask their husbands at home. For it is shameful for a woman to speak in church." And yet in each case, enlightened people have moved on from the worldview such passages express. . . .

And if science now teaches us that being gay may be a "natural" state, how can a reading of the Bible, including Saint Paul's condemnation of same-sex interaction in Romans, inarguably cast homosexuality in "unnatural" terms?

These are among the passages in letters attributed to Paul that many find more appalling than appealing. So we begin our story of Paul by speaking about his importance, the reasons for his mixed reputation, and the foundations for our way of seeing him.

Paul's importance is obvious from the New Testament itself. There are twenty-seven books in the New Testament, though to call them "books" is a bit of a misnomer, for some are only a page or a few pages long. Of these twenty-seven, thirteen are letters attributed to Paul. Not all were actually written by Paul, as we will soon report, but they bear his name. To these add the book of Acts, in which Paul is the main character in sixteen of its twenty-eight chapters. Thus half of the New Testament is about Paul.

Moreover, according to the New Testament, Paul was chiefly responsible for expanding the early Jesus movement to include Gentiles (non-Jews) as well as Jews. The result over time was a new religion, even though Paul (like Jesus) was a Jew who saw himself working within Judaism. Neither intended that a new religion would emerge in his wake.

This does not mean that Christianity is a mistake. But it does mean that the two most important foundational figures of Christianity were Jews whose passion was the God and the people of Israel. When Paul spoke to non-Jews, it was to the God of Israel as disclosed in Jesus to whom he called them. Nevertheless, Paul more than any other figure in the New Testament was responsible for the emergence of Christianity as a new religion that, though it included Jews, became increasingly separated from Judaism.

Paul's importance extends beyond the New Testament into the history of Christianity. Many of its most important theologians and reformers were decisively shaped by Paul's letters. St. Augustine (354–430) was converted to Christianity by a passage from Paul. Before his conversion he was a gifted, brilliant, and troubled young man who fathered a child with a woman to whom he was not married. His spiritual journey led him through philosophy to Manicheanism, a religion that emphasized that the flesh was bad and spirit was good.

Then one day, as Augustine tells the story, he heard a child singing, "Pick it up, read it." He picked up a copy of the New Testament, and his eyes fell upon Romans 13:13–14:

> Let us live . . . not in reveling and drunkenness, not in debauchery and licentiousness, not in quarreling and jealousy. Instead, put on the Lord Jesus Christ . . .

In his *Confessions,* commonly seen as the world's first spiritual autobiography, he reports:

> Instantly, as the sentence ended, there was infused in my heart something like the light of full certainty and all of the gloom of doubt vanished away.

After this experience mediated by Paul, Augustine became the most influential theologian of the first millennium of Christianity.

In the more than thousand years from Augustine to the Protestant Reformation of the sixteenth century, Paul continued to be revered because his writings were part of Christian sacred scripture. But during the Reformation, he became decisively important for Protestants. Martin Luther (1483–1546) had his transforming experience of radical grace while preparing lectures on Paul. Paul became the foundation of his theology, especially the Pauline contrasts between grace and law, and faith and works, language that has been paradigmatically important for Lutherans ever since.

John Calvin (1509–64), the other most important Protestant Reformer, also made Paul central to his theology. Calvin's theological descendants include millions of Protestants: Puritans, Presbyterians, Baptists, Congregationalists (today's United Church of Christ), and other Reformed denominations.

Two centuries later, Paul played a central role in the birth of the Methodist church. Its founder, John Wesley (1703–91), was converted to his mission to reform the Church of England while listening to a reading of Luther's commentary on Paul's letter to the Romans. His life's work eventually led to a new denomination, now the second largest Protestant denomination in America. Thus hundreds of millions of Protestants around the world, whether they know it or not, have Paul as their primary theological ancestor.

To say the obvious, Paul matters. But how he matters and how much he matters vary greatly among Christians. There are very diverse understandings of Paul's importance, message, and character. To some extent, the same could be said of Jesus, for he is diversely interpreted as well. But all Christians agree that Jesus was admirable, attractive, and appealing. Not so with Paul.

THE CATHOLIC PAUL AND
THE PROTESTANT PAUL

Catholics and Protestants see Paul's importance quite differently. For Protestants (at least historically—we're not sure about the present), an interpretation of Paul's theology and language is foundational for understanding Christianity. Not so for Catholics. Though they see Paul as a saint and his letters as sacred scripture, they have not made Paul central in the way that Protestants have. This difference can easily be seen in the history of Protestant and Catholic theology since the Reformation. But we illustrate it by speaking autobiographically.

Borg: In the Lutheran form of Christianity in which I grew up, Paul was more important than Jesus. Of course, none of my pastors or Sunday school teachers ever said this. Indeed, they would be puzzled by the statement. But as I look back on my experience of growing up Lutheran, it is clear that I was taught to see Jesus, God, and the Christian gospel through a Pauline lens as mediated by Luther. I was blissfully unaware of this, of course. I took it for granted that *our* way of seeing Jesus, God, and Christianity was not *a* way of seeing them, but *the* way.

For me as a Lutheran, the foundational Christian message was "justification by grace through faith," a Pauline and Lutheran phrase often shortened to "justification by faith." What this meant to me was that I would be accepted by God "by faith"— and faith meant believing in Jesus and God as understood by Paul and Luther.

Not until I went to seminary in my early twenties did I realize how Lutheran my way of seeing Paul and the gospel was. Not that the Lutheran view is simply wrong—it's much better than some. But I learned that there are other vantage points for seeing Paul, some that add greatly to his richness and fullness.

In another seminary decades later, I encountered the difference between Catholic and Protestant perceptions of Paul firsthand. While I was a visiting professor of New Testament in a theological consortium that included three Catholic seminaries, a number of Catholic students attended my courses. As I was lecturing about Paul's understanding of justification by grace, I noticed that several of the Catholic students looked puzzled, and then one asked, "What's all this about 'justification by grace'? Why is this important?" I realized that the phrase was largely foreign to them. Their puzzlement did not reflect theological naiveté, but the different significance of Paul for Protestants and Catholics.

Crossan: I, on the other hand, grew up blissfully unaware of those battling interpretations of Paul or even of the fierce Reformation controversies about him. As a Catholic, I knew him first as the latter half of a June 29 feast day dedicated to Sts. Peter and Paul, and my memory says that in the Ireland of the late 1930s and early 1940s that was a Holy Day of Obligation—like a Sunday. Then, in 1945, in a classical boarding school in Ireland, I ran into "Romulus et Remus" and realized that the twin heroes of pagan Rome had been displaced by "Petrus et Paulus," the twin heroes of Christian Rome—the double *R* ceding smoothly to the double *P*—with both individuals always in that given order.

Next, in 1959, when I first stood in St. Peter's Square in Rome and looked at the statues of St. Peter (on the basilica's primary, or gospel, side) and St. Paul (on its secondary, or epistle, side), I realized that their unity was as apostles martyred together in Rome. Paul was not there as an author or a theologian, but as a martyr. But, of course, while Peter held his keys, Paul did not hold his epistles.

I knew, by then, that there was already tension between Peter and Paul within the New Testament itself. Paul accused Peter "to his face" of "hypocrisy"—twice (Gal. 2:11–13). And, later, an author writing in Peter's name noted that "our beloved brother Paul wrote to you according to the wisdom given him . . . in all his letters. There are some things in them hard to understand, which the ignorant and unstable twist to their own destruction, as they do the other scriptures" (2 Pet. 3:15–16). So those twin Roman statues in front of St. Peter's represented a visual reconciliation of a process that went back to the fourth century, when Peter and Paul were emphasized together as the martyred founders of the new Christian Rome (match that, Constantinople!).

Finally, then, I conclude with an iconic image of that foundational reconciliation from the later fourth century. It is a bronze hanging lamp from the villa of the aristocratic Valerii on the Celian Hill in Rome, now preserved in the National Archaeological Museum in Florence. The lamp is shaped like a boat. Peter is seated in the stern at the tiller. Paul is standing in the prow looking forward. Peter steers. Paul guides. And the boat sails full before the wind.

In coauthoring this book in the "Year of Paul," June 29, 2008, to June 29, 2009, as proclaimed by Pope Benedict XVI, our common hope is that we can get Paul out of the Reformation world and back into the Roman world, to see him properly as contrasting not Christianity to Judaism or Protestantism to Catholicism, but Jewish covenantal traditions to Roman imperial theology.

Even though Protestants agree about Paul's importance, they see his message very differently. Two visions are especially divergent. For some, Paul has been a mediator of radical grace, unconditional grace—grace without conditions. So it was for Luther. Paul's message of justification by grace through faith brought about a joyous liberation from his anxious effort to be right with God by meeting God's requirements, a fear-filled task that tormented him into his thirties. Radical grace meant for Luther that God accepts us just as we are, and the Christian life is about living more and more fully into this realization, not about measuring up to requirements. For Luther, Paul's message was about the end of requirements as the basis of our relationship with God.

For other Protestants, including even many descendants of Luther, Paul's theology has been understood not as the abolition of requirements, but as the new requirement—namely, believing his theology is what we must do in order to be saved. In its Lutheran form, despite the emphasis upon God's grace, "justification by grace through faith" was heard as "justification by faith" and thus as involving a fearful form of works righteousness: the "work" was "to believe." Faith meant believing in a correct set of doctrines (which happened to be Lutheran), and this was the gateway to salvation. What Luther experienced as joyful liberation from anxiety became the source of deep anxiety. Faith—believing—became the new requirement we are to fulfill and by which we are to measure up.

This notion—that we are saved by believing a set of teachings about Jesus, God, and the Bible—continues among many Protestants in our time. It is especially prevalent among those who emphasize "believing the right things" as foundational to being Christian and thus as a requirement for salvation.

PAUL THE SPOILER

In addition to those with divergent interpretations of Paul that are positive, a growing number of Christians have a negative impression of him. For some, the reason is the difficulty of reading and understanding Paul's letters. They are very unlike the gospels, which are full of stories and memorable teachings. Rather, as letters written to Christian communities that had already been taught about Jesus, they do not often refer to his message and teaching. They strike many readers as "theological" in the negative sense of the word—as abstract rather than concrete, wordy rather than memorable.

Moreover, Paul's letters deal with local matters in these communities, including their questions and conflicts, and so they do not make much sense unless we know the local context in some detail. When we read Paul, we are reading somebody else's mail—and unless we know the situation being addressed, his letters can be quite opaque.

A third reason was mentioned at the beginning of this chapter; namely, passages from letters attributed to Paul endorse slavery, subordinate women, and condemn homosexual behavior. They have been used for much of Christian history to justify systems of oppression. As recently as a hundred and fifty years ago, some Christians used passages from Paul to defend slavery. Howard Thurman, a well-known twentieth-century African American pastor, theologian, and mystic, reported that his mother, a deeply devout Christian, would not read Paul because of the passages on slavery.

The subordination of women within the church and society lasted even longer than slavery. Only in the last forty years did most mainline Protestant denominations begin to ordain women as clergy. The Catholic church does not, most conservative Protestant churches do not, and many teach the subordination of wives to husbands. For these positions, passages from Paul's letters provide the primary justification. And the condemnation of homosexuality continues in many churches. Even within churches in which the attitude toward homosexuality is changing, the change often causes conflict.

Thus Paul has been used to support systems of cultural conventions oppressive to more than half of the human race. No wonder slaves, women, gays and lesbians, and those who care about them have often found Paul appalling.

In addition, we note a passage from Paul, not mentioned in the *Newsweek* article, that has been used in a comprehensive way to justify systems of oppression. The full passage is Romans 13:1–7; we quote its well-known opening lines:

> Let every person be subject to the governing authorities; for there is no authority except from God, and those authorities that exist have been instituted by God. Therefore whoever resists authority resists what God has appointed, and those who resist will incur judgment.

In the familiar and succinct phrase from an older translation, a portion of the first verse reads, "The powers that be are ordained by God." For centuries, this passage was used by Christian rulers to legitimate their rule and to demand obedience to it. Ordinary Christians understood it to require political quiescence.

We will return to this passage in Chapter 4. For now we note that during World War II, many German Christians used this passage to justify obedience to the Third Reich. Closer to our own time and place, many Christians in this country used it to oppose civil disobedience during the civil rights movement. More recently, a number of well-known evangelical preachers used it to legitimate supporting the American government's decision to invade Iraq: Christians are to obey their governments, whatever they do. But this is increasingly unpersuasive to many Christians.

Beyond these passages, some see Paul not simply as being wrong about specific issues in specific verses, but as the "spoiler" who pervasively distorted the message of Jesus. Several books, some written by scholars, argue that Paul changed the teaching and message *of* Jesus into a set of abstract doctrines *about* Jesus, and thus transformed the religion *of* Jesus into a religion *about* Jesus. For these, Paul was wrong not just in a few passages, but comprehensively. Jesus is good, but Paul is bad.

We do not share these negative views of Paul, even as we are quite willing to say he was wrong about some things. To see Paul positively does not mean endorsing everything he ever wrote.

But we are among his admirers. We see him as an appealing apostle of Jesus whose vision of life "in Christ"—one of his favored phrases—is remarkably faithful to the message and vision of Jesus himself. When we take into account the different circumstances of their activity—Jesus addressing Jews living in the Jewish homeland and Paul addressing Jews and Gentiles in the cities of the Roman Empire beyond the Jewish homeland— Paul emerges as a faithful apostle of the radical Jesus who became his Lord. For many people, meeting this Paul will be like meeting Paul again for the first time.

MEETING PAUL AGAIN

We begin by placing Paul in time and space. In Chapter 3, we will treat the life of Paul in some detail. For now, we provide some markers, beginning with Jesus.

Jesus was born around 4 BCE, possibly a year or two earlier. In the late 20s, he began his public activity and was soon executed by Roman imperial authority, most likely in the year 30 CE.

We don't know when Paul was born, but the most probable guess is the first decade of the first century. The basis for the guess is simple. Paul lived, and lived robustly, into the 60s of the first century. It is unlikely that he was in his seventies or eighties by then. Thus, Paul and Jesus were roughly contemporary, Paul not much younger than Jesus.

Though both were Jewish, they grew up in very different settings: Jesus in a small Jewish village in Galilee; Paul in Tarsus, a significant city in southern Asia Minor, modern-day Turkey. Jesus lived his life in the Jewish homeland. Paul was a product of the Jewish "Diaspora," a term referring to Jewish communities outside of the homeland.

We first hear of Paul in Acts a few years after Jesus's crucifixion. In Acts 7, in Jerusalem, he is present at the killing by stoning of a follower of Jesus named Stephen, commonly spoken of as the first Christian martyr. The story of Stephen's martyrdom ends in Acts 8:1 with the terse comment: "And Saul approved of their killing him." Saul—his name would be changed to Paul after his conversion—was probably in his twenties and almost certainly not much over thirty.

We next hear of him in Acts 9. Still named Saul, he is now himself persecuting followers of Jesus. Then, three to five years after Jesus's death, Saul had a life-changing experience of the risen Christ near or in Damascus in Syria. It transformed him from Saul, the persecutor of Jesus, to Paul, the apostle of Jesus to the Gentiles. For about twenty-five years thereafter, on foot and by sea, Paul traversed the eastern Roman Empire, mostly in Asia Minor and Greece, finally ending up in Rome. There, according to Christian tradition, he was executed, most likely in the early 60s.

During his lifetime, the written gospels did not yet exist. The first gospel, Mark, was written around the year 70, and the other three gospels in the New Testament—Matthew, Luke, and John—in the final decades of the first century. Paul's genuine letters, most or all written during the 50s, are thus the earliest writings in the New Testament.

With this chronology in mind, we turn now to the foundations of the way of seeing Paul that we develop in this book. They are not peculiar to us, but shared by mainstream New Testament scholarship—by which we mean the kind of scholarship taught in nonsectarian universities and colleges as well as seminaries of mainline denominations.

What differentiates mainstream scholars from fundamentalist and many conservative scholars is that the former do not begin with the presumption that the Bible is unlike other books in that it has a divine guarantee to be inerrant and infallible. Rather, mainstream scholars see the Bible as a historical product that can be studied as other historical documents are, without specifically Christian theological convictions shaping the outcome.

It is the approach described by the contemporary Catholic scholar John Meier, who begins his multivolume study of the historical Jesus by asking us to imagine four highly competent historians, all specialists in the study of Christian origins—a Catholic, a Protestant, a Jew, and an atheist—locked in a library until they can arrive at a consensus statement about Jesus. What could they agree on? What they could agree on, of course, would be those matters about which their specific religious beliefs would not be the deciding factor. It might not be much, but it would be foundational.

In this approach, three foundational statements form the basis of our way of seeing Paul. First, not all of the letters attributed to Paul were written by him—there is *more than one Paul* in the New Testament. Second, it is essential to place his letters in their *historical context*. Third, his message—his teaching, his gospel—is grounded in his life-changing and sustaining experience of the risen Christ; Paul, we will argue, is best understood as a *Jewish Christ mystic*.

THREE PAULS

Mainstream scholarship as it has developed over the last two centuries has concluded that the thirteen letters attributed to

Paul fall into three categories: letters written by Paul, those *not* written by him, and ones about which there is uncertainty. According to a massive scholarly consensus, at least seven letters are "genuine"—that is, written by Paul himself. These seven include three longer ones (Romans, 1 and 2 Corinthians) and four shorter ones (1 Thessalonians, Galatians, Philippians, and Philemon). Written in the 50s of the first century, plus or minus a year or two, they are the earliest documents in the New Testament, earlier than the gospels (recall that Mark, the first gospel, was written around 70). Thus the genuine letters of Paul are the oldest witness we have to what was to become Christianity.

According to an almost equally strong consensus, three letters were not written by Paul: 1 and 2 Timothy and Titus, commonly known as the "pastoral letters" or simply the "pastorals." Scholars estimate that they were written around the year 100, possibly a decade or two later. These are seen as "non-Pauline" because they have what looks like a later historical setting and a style of writing quite unlike Paul's in the seven genuine letters. Thus the letters to Timothy and Titus were written in the name of Paul several decades after his death. In case some readers may think that writing in somebody else's name was dishonest or fraudulent, we note that it was a common practice in the ancient world. It was a literary convention of the time, including within Judaism.

The third group, letters about which there is no scholarly consensus, are, however, seen by a majority as *not* coming from Paul. Often called the "disputed" letters, they include Ephesians, Colossians, and 2 Thessalonians. We are among those who see these as "post-Paul," written a generation or so after his death, midway between the genuine letters and the later pastoral letters.

Thus there are three "Pauls" within the letters attributed to him. To give names to these "Pauls," we call the Paul of the seven genuine letters the *radical Paul*. We call the Paul of the three pastoral letters the *reactionary Paul,* for the author of these letters is not simply developing Paul's message, but countering it at important points. What we see, as we shall illustrate in Chapter 2, is a strong accommodation of Paul's thought to the conventional mores of his contemporary time. In comparison to the radical Paul, we name the Paul of the disputed letters as the *conservative Paul.*

Our purpose is not to raise a debate about the use of terms like "radical," "reactionary," and "conservative." Rather, it is to insist that the post-Pauline, pseudo-Pauline letters are anti-Pauline with regard to major aspects of his theology. They represent, as we argue in the next chapter, a taming of Paul, a domestication of Paul's passion to the normalcy of the Roman imperial world in which he and his followers lived.

We do not want to complicate matters too much by introducing a *fourth Paul,* but the nature of our sources requires it. As mentioned earlier, over half of the book of Acts is about Paul. By the same author who wrote the gospel of Luke, Acts was most likely written near the end of the first century, some thirty years or so after Paul's death.

The literary form of Acts is very different from that of the letters, for it is a narrative—indeed, the only narrative about Paul that we have in the New Testament. It focuses more on Paul's activity than on his message. In it are the stories of Paul's conversion to be a follower of Jesus, told three times; his three missionary journeys; and his arrest in Jerusalem, imprisonment, and appearances before a variety of officials. Then he is taken to Rome as a prisoner to make his appeal to the emperor. Acts ends with Paul under house arrest in the capital of the empire, still preaching the gospel.

Because Acts does not report Paul's death, some scholars have argued that Acts must have been written while Paul was still alive, which would mean the early 60s at the latest. This argument presumes that the purpose of Acts was to provide a "life of Paul" and that the most plausible explanation for the lack of mention of Paul's death is that he hadn't yet died. But the purpose of Acts, the plan of the book, is to tell the story of the spread of the gospel from Jerusalem to Rome (see, for example, Acts 1:8). And so Acts ends appropriately with Paul preaching the gospel in the capital of the empire. For the author to have ended with, "And then Rome executed him," would have been an odd climax, to say the least.

To return to the question of the use of Acts as a source for Paul, there is significant scholarly disagreement about the degree to which the portrait of Paul in Acts is consistent with or different from the radical Paul of the genuine letters. Acts reports much that Paul's letters do not. This is neither surprising nor particularly significant, given the different literary genres. However, when there is overlap between Acts and the letters, Acts is sometimes consistent with the letters and sometimes not, making it difficult to assess the historical accuracy of Acts when there is *no* overlap.

Some scholars think that Acts and the letters can be harmonized quite nicely. Others argue that there are major differences. Because of this disagreement, we will not use Acts as a primary source for Paul, but as an important secondary source. Our primary source will be the seven genuine letters, supplemented when appropriate by Acts. We will have much more to say on this subject in Chapter 3.

HISTORICAL CONTEXT

Our second foundational concept is also shared in common with mainstream scholarship. It is the basis of all historical study of ancient texts, namely, the importance of setting texts within historical context. What was going on at the time? What were the circumstances that the author addressed? What did the author's words and allusions mean in their ancient historical and literary setting? Without context, one can imagine that a text means almost anything.

The context of Paul's letters involves a set of concentric circles. The center circle is the context of the communities to which he wrote. This is set within and surrounded by the context of the early Jesus movement, which is set within the context of Judaism, which is set within the context of the Roman Empire.

Though we know most of his letters by the names of cities, Paul was not writing to cities, but to small communities of early followers of Jesus within them—in Thessalonica, Corinth, and Philippi in Greece; Galatia in Asia Minor; and in Rome itself. The one genuine letter addressed to an individual, Philemon, was also meant for a wider group, for it was to be read to the community. In these letters written to Christian communities, Paul's purpose was not to proclaim the message of and about Jesus as a whole. The recipients of his letters had already been instructed about that.

Moreover, with the exception of Rome, Paul had been active in these communities. His letters were written to people he knew, and for the most part they addressed questions or problems that had arisen in these communities in his absence. They are "conversations in context," to use a phrase from the contemporary Paul scholar Calvin Roetzel, conversations in the context of Paul's relationship to these communities. To understand them requires setting them in the context of this conversation.

The second concentric context is the early Jesus movement, a phrase commonly used by scholars to name the followers of Jesus in the first decades after his death. The use of this phrase recognizes that calling them "Christians," as if they had become members of a new religion distinct from Judaism, is anachronistic.

According to Acts 9:2, they were known as followers of "the Way," the way of Jesus. However, despite the risk of anachronism, we will sometimes call them "Christians" or "Christian Jews" or "Christian Gentiles."

After Paul's dramatic experience of the risen Christ, he became part of the movement. Though Paul knew enough about Jesus before his Damascus experience to become a persecutor of his followers, his transformation into an apostle of Jesus involved learning more about Jesus from those who were part of the movement. It is intrinsically what we would expect, and Acts does in fact report it. Moreover, Paul was sustained by his involvement with Christian communities. As the contemporary scholar Peter Berger puts it, Saul became Paul in a moment of religious ecstasy; but Paul could remain Paul only in the context of Christian community. In his life as an apostle, Paul sought to express in the larger Mediterranean world what the Jesus movement meant for both Jews and Gentiles.

The third concentric contextual circle is first-century Judaism. Like Jesus, Paul was passionately Jewish. Jewish scripture (for Christians, the Old Testament) and Jewish practice shaped his life and thought, both before and after he became a follower of Jesus. Indeed, to the end of his life, Paul thought of himself as Jewish, not as having converted to a new religion. Without an understanding of Paul's Jewish context, much in his letters is opaque.

The fourth concentric contextual circle is the Roman Empire. Though it is not more important than the other circles, it is the largest and most comprehensive context. Paul and all of his communities lived under Roman rule.

This matters not simply as information about Paul's time and place. Rather, it matters because Roman rule was legitimated by an imperial theology that proclaimed that the emperor was the

Son of God, Lord, Savior of the World, and the one who had brought peace on earth. It also proclaimed, as we will see especially in Chapter 4, that peace and justice came through military victory and imperial order.

For now, we simply note that Paul's proclamation of Jesus as Son of God, Lord, and Savior directly countered Roman imperial theology. For Paul as a follower of Jesus, God as known in Jesus was Lord, and the emperor was not. In this context, Paul's most concise affirmation about Jesus—"Jesus is Lord"—was high treason. It is not surprising that Paul, like Jesus, was eventually executed by Rome.

In this fourfold context, much of what is in Paul's letters becomes luminous. Though the meaning of some passages remains uncertain, either because we don't know enough about the circumstances or because Paul was sometimes unclear, his genuine letters generate an understanding of Paul and his message that is remarkably consistent with the message of Jesus. Paul's message challenged the normalcy of civilization, then and now, with an alternative vision of how life on earth can and should be. The radical Paul, we are convinced, was a faithful follower of the radical Jesus.

A JEWISH CHRIST MYSTIC

In the rest of this book we will be discussing Paul's life and letters, mission and theology. But here, immediately, we emphasize the most important foundational fact about him: Paul was a Jewish Christ mystic.

We begin with the word "mystic" and its cousins "mystical" and "mysticism." Because of their diverse and ambiguous connotations in contemporary culture, they need explanation. The most common connotation of these words in popular usage is dismissive. To say something "sounds mystical" or "sounds like mysticism" means you don't need to take it seriously. It is something vague, fuzzy, ungrounded, perhaps otherworldly, and irrelevant.

In the academic world, the term is not dismissive, but ambiguous. It is used by some scholars in a very narrow and precise sense and by others in a much broader sense. Those who define it very narrowly see it as an unusual and very specific religious phenomenon. They see mysticism within Judaism and Christianity as a postbiblical development and would not use the terms "mystic" or "mysticism" for anything stemming from as early as the biblical period.

We are among those who define it more broadly. In five words, which of course need to be expanded, *mysticism is union with God.* A mystic is one who lives in union or communion with God. The difference between union and communion is relatively minor: the first involves a sense of "one-ness" with God; the second, a sense of connection with the sacred that is deep, close, and intimate, even though a sense of "two-ness" remains.

Most mystics have mystical experiences—by which we mean ecstatic experiences in which there is a vivid sense of the presence of God, or the Sacred, or the Real, terms that we use interchangeably here. An ecstatic experience, as the roots of the Greek word suggest, is a nonordinary state of consciousness. One is "out of" or "beyond" ordinary consciousness and in this state has an overwhelming sense of experiencing God. God becomes an experiential reality. In this sense, mystics *know* God. They do not simply believe in God, but have moved from believing to knowing.

A century ago, William James in *The Varieties of Religious Experience* provided the classic broad definition of mystical experiences. Such experiences, he said, involve a vivid sense of *union* and *illumination*. Since we have just spoken about the former, we turn to the latter.

"Illumination" has more than one connotation in the context of mystical experiences. The experiences often involve light. Sometimes they involve seeing light or a being of light—a *photism,* to use James's word. They can also involve seeing the world as radiant, as full of light. The earth is "full of God's glory" (Isa. 6:3), that is, full of the radiant luminosity of the sacred. Because the light sometimes becomes yellow or golden in these experiences, Mircea Eliade, the twentieth century's best-known scholar of comparative religions, called them "experiences of the golden world."

"Illumination" has yet another connotation in the context of mystical experiences. They often include a sense of "enlightenment," a vivid sense of seeing more clearly than one ever has before. And what one sees is "the way things are." To use another word from William James, they are *noetic*—they involve a strong sense of *knowing,* and not simply ecstatic feeling. People who have such experiences experience a radical perceptual shift— they see differently.

Enlightenment as a transformed way of seeing is not only part of mystical experience, but continues afterward. Common images speak of this as like moving from darkness to light, from blindness to sight, from sleeping to being awake. Thus, for example, the Buddha after his mystical experience under the Bo tree, became the "enlightened one," the "awakened one." In the New Testament, the same effect is spoken of with the image of blindness and sight in a verse familiar from the hymn "Amazing Grace": "I once was blind, but now I see" (see also John 9). Seeing is transformed; mystics see differently because of what they have seen.

In this broad sense of the word, texts in both Acts and Paul's letters show that Paul was a mystic. On this crucial foundational fact, Acts and Paul agree. (Later, in Chapter 3, we will also see certain differences between them.) According to Acts, Paul had a mystical experience of Jesus that was the transformative event of his life. It changed him from Saul the persecutor of Jesus to Paul the proclaimer of Jesus. In Acts, it happened on the "road to Damascus," a phrase that has entered popular language to describe a radical, life-changing experience. We refer to it in shorthand as Paul's Damascus experience.

The author of Acts tells the story three times, once as part of his narration (Acts 9) and twice in speeches attributed to Paul (Acts 22; 26). There are differences in details, such as what the men traveling with Paul experienced, which rules out taking the three accounts as exact factual reporting. Obviously the author of Acts was not concerned with factual inerrancy, or he would have harmonized the three stories. But on the main points the accounts agree: Paul saw a great light; he heard a voice and addressed it as "Lord"; the voice identified itself as Jesus; and the experience transformed him.

We illustrate with the first and fullest story. Paul was on his way from Jerusalem to Damascus in Syria to find followers of Jesus and bring them bound to Jerusalem. Then:

> As Paul was going along and approaching Damascus, suddenly a light from heaven flashed around him. He fell to the ground and heard a voice saying to him, "Saul, Saul, why do you persecute me?" He asked, "Who are you, Lord?" The reply came, "I am Jesus, whom you are persecuting." (Acts 9:3–5)

Paul experienced "a light from heaven," a *photism,* to use William James's term. He also heard a voice, what James calls an *audition,* sometimes but not always part of a mystical experience.

Paul addressed the light and the voice as "Lord" and asked, "Who are you?" This suggests that Paul had not seen a visual figure, but a light, as the text itself says. Then the voice announced, "I am Jesus," identifying the light as Jesus. Of course, this is the post-Easter Jesus, the risen Christ; the historical Jesus, the pre-Easter Jesus, had been dead for at least a few years.

As the story continues, the theme of illumination appears again. The light was so brilliant that it blinded Paul (Acts 9:9). Then, three days later, he was led to a Christian Jew in Damascus named Ananias. Ananias laid his hands on Paul and said, "The Lord Jesus, *who appeared to you* on your way here, has sent me so that you may regain your sight and be filled with the Holy Spirit. *And immediately something like scales fell from his eyes, and his sight was restored*" (Acts 9:17–18; all italics in biblical quotations have been added). Paul now saw differently—the light that was Jesus, and the Spirit with which he was now filled, had brought enlightenment: "something like scales fell from his eyes, and his sight was restored."

The story in Acts 9 ends with Paul being baptized, the early Christian rite of incorporation. Paul had become "in Christ," as he puts it in his letters. "In Christ" was for Paul a new identity that involved a new community and way of being.

So decisive was this experience that it divided Paul's life into two parts, the pre-Damascus Paul and the post-Damascus Paul. Commonly called his conversion experience, it is and it is not, depending upon what we mean by "conversion." In a religious context, the word has three meanings, not all of which apply to Paul. The first is conversion from being nonreligious to being religious, the second is conversion from one religion to another, and the third is conversion within a religious tradition.

Paul's experience was neither of the first two. Clearly, he was deeply religious before his Damascus experience. In his own

words, he was filled with religious passion: "zealous for the traditions of my ancestors"; "as to the law, a Pharisee; as to zeal,
a persecutor of the church; as to righteousness under the law,
blameless" (Gal. 1:14; Phil. 3:5–6). Moreover, he did not convert
from one religion to another. Not only was Christianity not yet
a religion separate from Judaism, but Paul thought of himself as
a Jew after his conversion and for the rest of his life. Paul's was a
conversion within a tradition: from one way of being Jewish to
another way of being Jewish, from being a Pharisaic Jew to being
a Christian Jew.

Paul's Damascus experience was his "call" to the rest of his
life. It called him to his vocation, just as the "call stories" of the
great Jewish prophets were calls to a vocation. All three accounts
in Acts report that his Damascus experience was his commis-
sioning to his vocation as an apostle to the Gentiles.

Paul's genuine letters confirm the picture created by Acts.
Paul had experiences of Jesus as a living reality, and these experiences transformed him. We begin with Galatians 1:13–17, simply
because it is one of only two places in Paul's letters in which
he mentions Damascus. He describes his earlier life as a zealous
persecutor of the Jesus movement. Then he writes:

> God, who had set me apart before I was born and called
> me through his grace, was pleased to reveal his Son to
> me, so that I might proclaim him among the Gentiles.

In his own words, Paul testifies that he had an experience of divine revelation ("God was pleased to reveal his Son to me") that
transformed him and gave him his vocation. Two verses later,
in 1:17, he connects this experience to Damascus. After referring
to some subsequent events in his life, he says, "Afterwards, I returned to Damascus."

In other letters Paul also speaks of having experienced Jesus. He does so twice in 1 Corinthians. In 9:1, he says that he has "seen Jesus our Lord." Nothing in Acts or his letters suggests that Paul had ever seen the pre-Easter Jesus. The passage must refer to seeing the post-Easter Jesus—the risen Jesus as Christ and Lord.

Later in the same letter, he speaks of Jesus appearing to him. In 15:3–8, he names people to whom the risen Christ appeared and includes himself in the list: "He appeared also to me." Paul has had firsthand experience of the risen Christ—and, interestingly, one that he says belongs in a list of resurrection experiences had by Peter and other Christian apostles.

In 2 Corinthians (which may combine several letters), Paul says he "will go on to visions and revelations of the Lord." Note the plural: we should not imagine that the Damascus experience was his only experience of the risen Christ. Then he speaks of "a person in Christ who . . . was caught up to the third heaven." Though Paul uses third-person language here, he almost certainly refers to himself. "Such a person," he continues, "whether in the body or out of the body I do not know; God knows—was caught up into Paradise and heard things that are not to be told, that no mortal is permitted to repeat" (12:1–4).

The passage speaks of entering another level of reality ("the third heaven," "Paradise"), in an ecstatic state ("whether in the body or out of the body, I do not know"), where he heard "things that are not to be told." We do not think that the last phrase means secret information that could in principle be disclosed. Rather, it is best understood as something beyond words— "things unutterable," as an earlier translation put it. Again to use William James's language, this is mystical experience as ineffable—as impossible to put into words, as beyond words.

Another passage in the same letter uses the language of mysticism:

And all of us, with unveiled faces, seeing the glory of
the Lord as though reflected in a mirror, are being transformed into the same image from one degree of glory to
another; for this comes from the Lord, the Spirit. (2 Cor.
3:18)

"Unveiled faces" is a mystical image—the veil has been removed.
So also is "seeing the glory of the Lord," the radiant luminosity
of the Lord "as though reflected in a mirror" (see also 1 Cor.
13:12: "For now we see in a mirror, dimly"). The result is that we
"are being transformed."

All of these passages—and more could be cited—indicate
that Paul had mystical experiences of the risen Christ. He experienced the post-Easter Jesus as the light and glory of God, the
one who enlightened and transformed him.

Paul was not simply a mystic. More precisely, he was a *Jewish
Christ mystic*. He was a *Jewish* Christ mystic because, as already
mentioned, Paul was a Jew and in his own mind never ceased
being one. He was a Jewish *Christ* mystic because the content
of his mystical experiences was Jesus as risen Christ and Lord.
Afterward, Paul's identity became an identity "in Christ." And as
a Christ mystic, he saw his Judaism anew in the light of Jesus.

We cannot claim this foundation as a consensus view. Scholars
and theologians have often written about Paul without grounding his vocation and message as an apostle of Jesus in his mystical experience of the post-Easter Jesus. They have treated Paul's
letters as if they were primarily about a set of ideas that need to
be systematized and explained.

But our view is neither new nor idiosyncratic. A century ago,
the German New Testament scholar Adolf Gustav Deissman
wrote in his book *Paul: A Study in Social and Religious History*:
"Whoever takes away the mystical element from Paul, the man

of antiquity, sins against the Pauline word: 'Quench not the Spirit'" (1 Thess. 5:19). Deissman also affirmed that Paul's phrase "in Christ" (which occurs over a hundred times in the genuine letters) "is meant vividly and mystically, as is the corresponding 'Christ in me.'"[1] We explore these phrases in Chapters 5 and 7.

In addition to seeing Paul's mystical experience of the risen Christ as transforming him from a persecutor of Jesus's followers to a proclaimer of Jesus, there is one more crucial transformation to underline. And that is that his experience of the risen Christ transformed his perception of the authorities, the powers, that had crucified Jesus.

Paul's experience of the risen Christ carried with it the conviction that God had raised Jesus, that God had vindicated Jesus, that Jesus is Lord. But if God has vindicated Jesus, then the powers who killed him—Roman imperial authority in collaboration with Jewish high-priestly authority—are wrong. This sets up the fundamental opposition in Paul's theology. Who is Lord, Jesus or empire? In Paul, the mystical experience of Jesus Christ as Lord led to resistance to the imperial vision, and advocacy of a different vision of the way the world can be.

CHAPTER TWO

HOW TO READ A PAULINE LETTER

I<small>T IS WISE TO REMEMBER THAT</small>, when we are reading letters never intended for us, any problems of understanding are ours and not theirs. Sometimes, however, another person's mail is still clear to us even across two thousand years. Here is a letter discovered at Oxyrhynchus in Egypt and dated to "[Year] 29 of Caesar [Augustus], Payni 23," that is, for us, June 18 of 1 BCE:

> Hilarion to his sister Alis many greetings, likewise to my lady Berous and to Apollonarion. Know that we are even yet in Alexandria. Do not worry if they all come back (except me) and I remain in Alexandria. I urge and entreat you, be concerned about the child and if I should receive my wages soon, I will send them up to you. If by chance you bear a child, if it is a boy, let him be, if it is a girl, cast her out. You have said to Aphrodisias, "Do not forget me." How can I forget you? Therefore I urge you not to worry. (POxy 4.744)

Hilarion and others left their native Oxyrhynchus to work in Epypt's capital city of Alexandria. But, once there, Hilarion failed to write home. So his worried wife, Alis—who in Egyptian custom was also his sister—sent him a message with somebody called Aphrodisias. This is his reply from Alexandria. At the start of his letter he greets Alis, their mother Berous, and their son Apollonarion. We can also see quite clearly the terrible difference in this father's attitude toward having a son and having a daughter. A daughter is to be "cast out"—left either on temple steps, and destined for slavery, or on the garbage dump, and destined for death.

For a fuller understanding of that single letter today we would need: first, to study the letter itself; next, to place it within the life of that family; and, finally, to locate it in the wider cultural and social matrix of its contemporary Egypt. But even as we work through those interwoven layers of context, we are always trying to do just one thing: *to turn letter into story.* That original story was well known to all those originally mentioned in the letter, but— for us—a translation is necessary not only from Greek to English, but from letter to story. And that translation is developed by asking the letter questions, questions, and more questions.

Recall, therefore, that, as we said in Chapter 1, when we read Paul, we are reading somebody else's mail. The only way to understand a *Pauline letter* is to turn it into a *Pauline story* by working our way *through* the Pauline matrix of a single letter *within* all of his other letters *within* Diaspora Judaism *within* the Roman Empire.

In this chapter's first section, we do that for one of Paul's letters. We turn it from a letter back into the story well and fully understood by all originally concerned with it. Thereby we reconstruct its historical situation in order understand its theological function. We read through an entire letter, and you will be glad to know that the chosen text is the one-chapter letter to Philemon and not the sixteen-chapter letter to the Romans!

In this chapter's second section, we focus on the subject—slavery—of that chosen letter. We show how—on slavery—the *radical* Paul of the letter to Philemon is transformed, first, into the *conservative* "Paul" of the letters to Colossians and Ephesians and, then, into the *reactionary* "Paul" of the letter to Titus. We watch, within the New Testament itself, the historical Paul become the post-Paul, the pseudo-Paul, and the anti-Paul.

In this chapter's third and final section, we ask if the letter to Philemon is just a peculiar case with no implications for deeper Pauline theology and later post-Pauline tradition. In answer we look from Paul on slavery to Paul on patriarchy. And we show exactly the same transformation of Paul into anti-Paul with patriarchy as with slavery.

This chapter's conclusion is that the *radical* Paul opposes—and the *conservative* and *reactionary* "Pauls" accept—the normalcy of Roman hierarchy in its most obvious social expressions. This is our first insight into how *radical equality* within Pauline Christian theology opposes and replaces the *normal hierarchy* within Roman imperial theology. And the tragedy is that the Paul of the post-Pauline tradition is not only deradicalized; he is Romanized.

The letter chosen for our purpose is the only letter the historical Paul ever wrote to an individual person rather than to communities such as the Thessalonians, Galatians, Corinthians, Philippians, and Romans. Since it has only one chapter, we cite it simply by verse alone.

THE RADICAL PAUL ON SLAVERY

As we saw above, ancient letters begin in sender-to-recipient format more like the from-to style of our office memoranda than our personal letters, which address the recipient at the beginning and are signed by the sender at the end. And so Paul begins this letter:

> Paul, a prisoner of Christ Jesus, and Timothy our brother,
> To Philemon our dear friend and co-worker, to Apphia our sister, to Archippus our fellow soldier, and to the church in your house. (1–2)

The phrase "and Timothy" indicates that Timothy is the scribe-secretary to whom Paul dictated the letter. Notice the familial language of "brother" for Timothy and "sister" for Apphia (Philemon's wife?) and also the egalitarian language of "co-worker" for Philemon and "fellow soldier" for Archippus. But, above all else, notice the opening phrase, "Paul, a prisoner of Christ Jesus." That is our first focus.

Normally, as we will see with greater detail in Chapter 3, Paul opens his letters by identifying himself as an "apostle of Christ Jesus" (Gal. 1:1; 1 Cor. 1:1; 2 Cor. 1:1; Rom. 1:1). But here he is a "prisoner of Christ Jesus." Even in his letter to the Philippians—which is from the same imprisonment as the one in the letter to Philemon—Paul does not identify himself initially as a prisoner. He simply begins with "Paul and Timothy, servants of Christ Jesus" (1:1). So, "prisoner" (not "apostle" or "servant") is important for Paul here. Why?

On the one hand, Paul is free enough to write this letter, and in it he mentions seven people who are supporting him in prison: Timothy (1), Onesimus (13), Epaphras, Mark, Aristarchus, Demas, and Luke (23–24). On the other hand, in the letter's first half he mentions that he is a "prisoner" twice (1, 9) and refers to "during my imprisonment" twice (10, 13). It is actually that second reference that helps us understand more fully Paul's actual situation.

The phrase "during my imprisonment" is literally "in my chains" (Greek *en desmois*). That, by the way, is the same expression Paul uses in his letter to the Philippians, most likely written from this same imprisonment (1:7, 13, 14, 17). But what does "in chains" mean and what freedom of contact and support did it allow? To understand Paul's precise situation "in chains" in the early 50s, we detour through a similar "in chains" for another prisoner in the late 30s.

In 7 BCE, Aristobulus was executed by his father, Herod the Great, and his infant son, Agrippa, was reared in the imperial household at Rome with the future emperors Caligula and Claudius as his playmates. By 41 CE, Agrippa would have a territory and a title equal to that of his grandfather, Herod the Great, the Rome-appointed "King of the Jews." But he would only rule until 44, when, as Luke records tersely, "an angel of the Lord struck him down, and he was eaten by worms and died" (Acts 12:23).

In between, around 36–37 CE, when the emperor Tiberius was already in his late seventies, Agrippa prayed openly that Tiberius would soon be dead and Caligula emperor in his place. Josephus tells the tale briefly in *Jewish War* (2.179–180) and much more fully in *Jewish Antiquities* (18.168–237). When that comment was reported to Tiberius, he had Agrippa arrested and imprisoned pending a hearing. But other imperial patrons ensured

> that the soldiers who were to guard him and that the centurion who would be in charge of them and would also be handcuffed to him should be of humane character, that he should be permitted to bathe every day and receive visits from his freedmen and friends, and that he should have bodily comforts too. His friend Silas and two of his freedmen, Marsyas and Stoecheus, visited him

bringing him his favorite viands, and doing whatever service they could. They brought him garments that they pretended to sell, but, when night came, they made him a bed with the connivance of the soldiers. (18.203–4)

Here we see how a prisoner can be connected by chains (*desmoi*) to a soldier, but still be allowed the ministrations of his friends. And, finally, with Tiberius's timely death, Caligula "in exchange for his iron chain, gave him [Agrippa] a golden one of equal weight" (18.237). At times of dynastic transitions, high treason can be simply bad timing.

Being "in chains," attached to a soldier in the barracks while awaiting judgment, was a dangerous situation in which summary execution was possible at any moment. But even in that lethal situation—for Paul as for Agrippa—the prisoner could get whatever help and support he could afford from outside the prison. Think of bribery as part of the soldier's salary.

Finally, where was Paul imprisoned when he wrote to Philemon and to the Philippians? Both those letters came from the proconsular jail at Ephesus, capital of the Roman province of Asia Minor. When, for instance, Paul mentions "the whole imperial guard" in Philippians 1:13, the Greek is simply "in the whole praetorium," that is, throughout the governor's entire jail. Later, in 1 Corinthians, he writes that he "fought with wild animals at Ephesus" (15:32). That should be taken metaphorically, as one did not live to write about literally fighting in the arena with wild beasts.

That exact same metaphor was used over a half century later by Ignatius of Antioch in his *Epistle to the Romans*—and possibly used in imitation of Paul. "From Syria to Rome I am fighting with wild beasts, by land and sea, by night and day bound to ten 'leopards' [that is, a company of soldiers], and they become worse for kind treatment" (5:1). As he traveled to martyrdom in Rome, Ignatius was—like Paul—free to receive support and assistance from fellow Christians, free to write seven letters to churches along his route, but always chained to one or another of that military squad known as the "Leopards."

And so, after that explanatory detour, we return to Paul's letter to Philemon. After the names of sender and recipient, the protocols of an ancient letter required a greeting:

> Grace to you and peace from God our Father and the Lord Jesus Christ. (3)

In this greeting, the "you" is plural. But that phrase "grace and peace" appears as in the greeting of every single one of Paul's seven authentic letters. We will, therefore, leave it for now, but return to consider it in much greater detail in Chapter 4.

After the greeting Paul continues with his usual thanksgiving element:

> When I remember you in my prayers, I always thank my God because I hear of your love for all the saints and your faith toward the Lord Jesus. I pray that the sharing of your faith may become effective when you perceive all the good that we may do for Christ. I have indeed received much joy and encouragement from your love, because the hearts of the saints have been refreshed through you, my brother. (4–7)

Paul's thanksgiving verses usually interweave recipient, God, and Christ. Read, for example, what he says in 1 Thessalonians 1:2–3 and 1 Corinthians 1:4–9. And when Paul writes, for example, to the Philippians from the Ephesian prison, he says, "I thank my God every time I remember you, constantly praying with joy in every one of my prayers for all of you, because of your sharing in the gospel from the first day until now" (1:3–5).

At a first glance, therefore, this thanksgiving element in Philemon is not at all unusual. The "you" in the greeting is plural, but
in this thanksgiving the "you" is singular, focusing on Philemon
himself. Although the letter involves a personal matter, it is not a
private one. It also involves the twice mentioned "saints" (5, 7).

What makes this thanksgiving strikingly unusual is what comes
immediately after it. What follows it turns the thanksgiving into
what Latin rhetoric calls *captatio benevolentiae* ("capturing your
benevolence") and we might call "laying it on thick." It is like the
fulsome praise of a person's generosity that precedes a request
for a loan. For a moment think of yourself in Philemon's place.
You are first addressed as Paul's "dear friend and co-worker," then
praised for "your love for all the saints and your faith toward the
Lord Jesus," and finally termed "my brother." Then, as you bask
among those accolades, you are hit with this:

> For this reason, though I am bold enough in Christ to
> command you to do your duty, yet I would rather appeal
> to you on the basis of love—and I, Paul, do this as an old
> man, and now also as a prisoner of Christ Jesus. (8–9)

First, notice that, whether Paul commands or appeals, it is a
matter of Philemon's duty. Whatever *it* is, Philemon should do *it*
without any command or appeal from Paul or anyone else. Poor
Philemon is forced—abruptly and tersely—to face these three
words in this sequential relationship:

command ➤ DUTY ◂ appeal

It is not just a matter of Paul's appeal or command but,
before either option, a matter of Philemon's duty. Ouch!

Second, we now see—by its repetition (9)—why "prisoner"
was Paul's first mark of identification as the letter's sender (1).
How can Philemon possibly not do his duty, when Paul is so

clearly doing his? Notice that, each time, Paul is not just a "prisoner," but a "prisoner of Christ Jesus." That phrase has a magnificent and deliberate ambiguity—does that Greek genitive case ("of" in English) mean a prisoner *because of* Jesus or *by* Jesus? Is Paul a prisoner of Jesus because of Rome or a prisoner of Rome because of Jesus? "Think about that, dear Philemon," Paul is really saying. "And how, dear Philemon, can you refuse me who am not only a prisoner of Jesus Christ (1, 9), but also an old man (9)?" But we still do not know what *it* is—what is the "duty" Philemon must fulfill? What can he not refuse to do?

So Paul continues his letter:

> I am appealing to you for my child, Onesimus, whose father I have become during my imprisonment. Formerly he was useless to you, but now he is indeed useful both to you and to me. (10–11)

The link from 8–9 to 10–11 is very clear in Greek: "I would rather appeal to you" (*parakalō*) is the exact same word as "I am appealing to you" (*parakalō*). Paul is appealing to Philemon (to do his duty!) concerning somebody named Onesimus. We now—almost midway into the letter—hear his name for the first and only time.

The relationship between Onesimus and Paul is described as "child" and "father," a metaphor for convert and apostle. Onesimus, which means "useful" in Greek, is a common slave name. Paul uses that name to pun delicately about something Onesimus did that rendered him temporarily "useless" to his owner, Philemon.

Since Onesimus had clearly come to Paul without Philemon's permission, how exactly are we to imagine his situation? On the one hand, he is clearly a runaway slave. On the other, he has fled to the most dangerous place imaginable—to a Roman prisoner

in a Roman jail. Has he not endangered his own life and that of
Paul as well?

If we assume that Onesimus is not simply imprudent here,
there is another way to understand his action. When severe
punishment or even death was imminent, Roman law allowed a
slave to flee not only to certain temples for refuge, but also "to
a friend" (Latin *ad amicum*) of the owner to beg for intercession
and mercy.

An example will make this clear. Although Seneca the Younger
became a victim near the end of Nero's reign, he had begun it
as the young emperor's philosopher. He wrote the treatises *On
Mercy* and *On Anger* in the same decade that Paul wrote this letter
to Philemon (which might be called, as it were, *On Duty*). In the
former study, Seneca mentions that "Slaves have the right to seek
refuge at a god's statue" (1.18.2). In the latter one, he gives us this
story about a slave's (short) flight *ad amicum*.

The anecdote concerns what "our deified Augustus did when
dining with Vedius Pollio" at the latter's palatial mansion above
the Bay of Naples:

> One of the servants had broken a crystal cup. Vedius or-
> dered him to be seized and executed in an unusual way—
> he was to be thrown to the giant lampreys which were
> kept in a pool. . . . The boy struggled free and fled to
> Caesar's feet, asking only for some other form of death,
> just not to be eaten. Shocked by the unprecedented
> cruelty, Caesar had him released, ordering all the crystal
> to be broken in front of him and the pool to be filled in.
> (3.40.2–4)

Seneca notes that the slave fled "upward," fled to one who was
his owner's friend, but who could also operate "from a position
of superiority." That might be parable rather than history, but

when Pollio's will left that mansion to Augustus, the emperor had it demolished and turned into a garden.

Our best reconstruction of Onesimus's intention and situation is that he was in some very serious trouble with his owner, Philemon, and fled—legally by Roman law—for intercession to Paul, whom he recognized as the somewhat "superior" friend of his master. But now that original situation has changed, because the pagan slave has become a Christian convert. So what exactly is Philemon's duty in that changed situation? Is it to take him back as a forgiven and now Christian slave? Or to give him to Paul as the apostle's own slave? It is neither—but something much more radical.

Paul continues:

> I am sending him, that is, my own heart, back to you. I wanted to keep him with me, so that he might be of service to me in your place during my imprisonment for the gospel; but I preferred to do nothing without your consent, in order that your good deed might be voluntary and not something forced. (12–14)

So Paul is certainly not asking Philemon to leave Onesimus—enslaved or freed—with him at Ephesus. He sends him back as his "own heart." First, notice the bite in the phrase "in your place." Paul might as well be saying, "Onesimus was here to help me, and where were you, dear Philemon? Oh!"—with sarcasm—"Maybe he was here as your representative?" Second, as you might expect by now, it is a good time for another mention of "my imprisonment for the gospel"—literally, "in my chains of the gospel." That is the same deliberate ambiguity seen twice already—has Rome put Paul in chains because of the gospel or has the gospel put Paul in chains because of Rome? Finally, notice also, the phrase about Philemon's "good deed" being "voluntary and not something forced."

That takes us deep into the Pauline theology that insists on *faith-with-works* against *works-without-faith*. Do not confuse that, by the way, with the Reformation's pseudo-problem (yes, pseudo-problem) of *faith*-against-*works*, so useful for its polemical treatises on Christians against Jews and Protestants against Catholics. Philemon must free Onesimus freely as a work proceeding intrinsically from faith and not as a work proceeding extrinsically from enforced obedience to Paul. That is the reason for Paul's roller-coaster, up-and-down, praise-and-blame, good cop–bad cop rhetoric in this letter.

Paul continues:

> Perhaps this is the reason he was separated from you for a while, so that you might have him back forever, no longer as a slave but more than a slave, a beloved brother— especially to me but how much more to you, both in the flesh and in the Lord. (15–16)

There we finally have it—the "duty" and "good deed" is to free Onesimus freely. Philemon is not to free him out of necessity so that he can remain permanently with Paul; rather, Onesimus is to go home to voluntary liberation (manumission) from Philemon. Maybe, says Paul to Philemon, that is why this all happened— Onesimus was "separated" (does the passive voice here indicate agency by God?) from Philemon in slavery, so that he could return to him for freedom.

The phrase "both in the flesh and in the Lord" is a crucial element for understanding Paul's meaning. Philemon cannot keep Onesimus as a Christian slave by claiming that—inside, spiritually, in our souls—we are all equal before God and Christ. The equality of liberation must be both physical and social as well as spiritual and theological.

Paul continues and pushes home his point once again:

So if you consider me your partner, welcome him as
you would welcome me. If he has wronged you in any
way, or owes you anything, charge that to my account.
I, Paul, am writing this with my own hand: I will repay
it. I say nothing about your owing me even your own
self. (17–19)

Once again the bite of sarcasm is very obvious—as if Paul could
have an "account" payable to Philemon, who owes Paul his very
"own self" as a Christian. And, to make it worse, Paul writes this
verse himself in large letters as if he were signing off on a debt,
as if to say, "Maybe, dear Philemon, you require a signature to
make this all legal?" By this point, poor Philemon must have had
no idea what hit him. And remember that all of this is in a personal but public letter.

And Paul continues just as forcefully (to use a kind word):

Yes, brother, let me have this benefit from you in the
Lord! Refresh my heart in Christ. Confident of your obedience, I am writing to you, knowing that you will do
even more than I say. One thing more—prepare a guest
room for me, for I am hoping through your prayers to be
restored to you. (20–22)

Look closely at the rhythm of those three verses. The first one
is gentle (20). It addresses Philemon once again as "brother" and
mentions "refresh my heart," as if Paul is finishing up by referring back to those same words at the start of the letter (7). As you
will recall, that earlier verse was followed by Paul appealing to
rather than commanding Philemon (8–9).

But in the present three verses, the next verse, 21, rather annuls those earlier verses, 8–9. The phrase "confident of your
obedience" (21) annuls "though I am bold enough in Christ to

command you to do your duty, yet I would rather appeal to you on the basis of love" (8–9). So it is a command after all, but from whom? Paul or Christ or God or all of them? The third verse reverts once more to the language of friends and equals, but it also has a slight edge, as if to say: "Do not think, dear Philemon, that a proconsular jail means you will never see me again."

And in conclusion:

> Epaphras, my fellow prisoner in Christ Jesus, sends greetings to you, and so do Mark, Aristarchus, Demas, and Luke, my fellow workers. The grace of the Lord Jesus Christ be with your spirit. (23–25)

The letter's conclusion, like its opening, reiterates that the entire affair of Philemon and Onesimus is personal, but not private; it reminds Philemon that it is a public matter, and everyone is watching what he will do. Although we might tend to focus on Mark and Luke because of the gospels named after but not written by them, it is Epaphras who deserves our strongest interest.

Just as our names are often abbreviated from, say, Margaret to Maggie or James to Jim, so were ancient names. Paul shortened Luke's Priscilla (Acts 18:2, 18, 26) to Prisca (Rom. 16:3; 1 Cor. 16:19; 2 Tim. 4:19) and even within his own letters Epaphroditus (Phil. 2:25; 4:18) to Epaphras (Philem. 23).

While Paul was in the Ephesian prison, his Philippian converts had sent him financial help with Epaphroditus, who was also to stay and help him. But, writes Paul, "I think it necessary to send to you Epaphroditus—my brother and co-worker and fellow soldier, your messenger and minister to my need, . . . because he came close to death for the work of Christ, risking his life to make up for those services that you could not give me" (2:25, 30). What is the story behind the individual named Epaphroditus in Philippians 2:25–30; 4:18 and Epaphras in Philemon 23?

In the phrase describing Epaphras, "my fellow prisoner" (*sun-aichmalōtos*), the Greek is not the same as that used by Paul for himself as a "prisoner" (*desmios*) or "in chains" (*en desmois*) in those four verses of Philemon (1, 9, 10, 13). It is, however, the same word Paul uses for both Andronicus and Junia in Romans 16:7. Why this different word and what does it mean? In answer we take one final detour into the wider contextual matrix of Roman incarceration.

The second-century author Lucian, from Samosata on the upper Euphrates, wrote a satire on the life and death of a Christian named Peregrinus, who later converted to become a Cynic named Proteus. In his booklet *The Passing of Peregrinus* Lucian describes the support Peregrinus received during his Christian period while in a Syrian prison. He mentions that Christian "officials even slept inside with him after bribing the guards" (12). In that case, Lucian judges Peregrinus to be a hypocrite and the officials to be fools. His judgment is very different, however, when that happens not to a Christian believer, but to a pagan philosopher.

In *Toxaris,* or *Friendship,* Lucian tells a story—but this time with approval—of another prisoner aided during incarceration. The tale is about two friends, Demetrius, a philosopher, and Antiphilus, a doctor, in Egypt. Once, while Demetrius was away, Antiphilus was arrested unjustly for a sacrilegious temple robbery perpetrated by his slave Syrus. With no support or assistance from anyone, Antiphilus's imprisonment was quite terrible:

> His health was beginning to give way under the strain, and no wonder: his bed was the bare ground, and all night he was unable so much as to stretch his legs, which were then secured in the stocks; in the daytime, the collar and one manacle sufficed, but at night he had to submit to being bound hand and foot. The stench, too, and the closeness

of the dungeon, in which so many prisoners were huddled
together gasping for breath, and the difficulty of getting
any sleep, owing to the clanking of chains—all combined
to make the situation intolerable to one who was quite
unaccustomed to endure such hardships. (29)

That, by the way, gives us a glimpse of what jail would have been
like for Paul, were he not significant enough to be chained to a
soldier in the barracks and supported by the presence of at least
seven friends.

When Demetrius returned, he went straight to the prison,
found Antiphilus, and at first was allowed to minister to his needs.
He went to work as a porter in the harbor and gave half of his
wages to bribe the guard and half to help his friend. But then the
jailer forbade any more such visits for anyone, and Demetrius
had to make a dangerous decision:

> Demetrius . . . could think of no other means of obtaining
> access to his friend than by going to the Prefect and pro-
> fessing complicity in the temple robbery. As the result of
> this declaration, he was immediately led off to prison, and
> with great difficulty prevailed upon the jailer after many
> entreaties to place him next to Antiphilus, and under the
> same collar. It was now that his devotion to his friend ap-
> peared in the strongest light. Ill though he was himself,
> he thought nothing of his own sufferings: his only care
> was to lighten the affliction of his friend, and to procure
> him as much rest as possible; and the companionship in
> misery certainly lightened his load. (32)

That is no doubt the hyperbole of parable rather than the pre-
cision of history, but we have to imagine something similar—

if less extreme—with Epaphras and Paul. Epaphras chose to live inside the prison alongside Paul as if he were his personal slave—not as a fellow criminal prisoner (*sundesmios*), but as a fellow prison inmate (*sunaichmalōtos*), accepting freely all the dangers to health and even life entailed in that decision. When you read the letter to Philemon, therefore, do not think only about Onesimus; think also of Epaphras (Epaphroditus).

THE CONSERVATIVE PAUL
ON SLAVERY

Imagine, for a moment, the domestic situation when Onesimus arrived home with that letter for Philemon and announced that there was good news and bad news or, better, that the good news for him was bad news for his owner. (We do not, by the way, presume that their city was Colossae, despite the pseudo-Pauline letter to the Colossians, 4:9).

Onesimus's liberation could not have been kept a secret. What if Philemon had other slaves—would there have been an immediate mass conversion to Christianity? What rumors would have spread throughout the slave infrastructure of their village or city about Christians? Critics could easily have accused Christians—unfairly, but maybe inevitably—of advising slaves to flee their owners or even murder them in their beds. Still, even granted all of that, it is surely sad that the radical Paul of the letter to Philemon was so swiftly and thoroughly sanitized into the conservative Paul of Colossians and Ephesians.

In both those books, pseudo-Paul addresses Christian slaves and Christian slave owners and thereby depicts those relationships as perfectly normal. Here are the texts, with Ephesians probably based on Colossians:

Slaves, obey your earthly masters in everything, not only while being watched and in order to please them, but wholeheartedly, fearing the Lord. Whatever your task, put yourselves into it, as done for the Lord and not for your masters, since you know that from the Lord you will receive the inheritance as your reward; you serve the Lord Christ. For the wrongdoer will be paid back for whatever wrong has been done, and there is no partiality.

Masters, treat your slaves justly and fairly, for you know that you also have a Master in heaven. (Col. 3:22–4:1)

Slaves, obey your earthly masters with fear and trembling, in singleness of heart, as you obey Christ; not only while being watched, and in order to please them, but as slaves of Christ, doing the will of God from the heart. Render service with enthusiasm, as to the Lord and not to men and women, knowing that whatever good we do, we will receive the same again from the Lord, whether we are slaves or free.

And, *masters,* do the same to them. Stop threatening them, for you know that both of you have the same Master in heaven, and with him there is no partiality. (Eph. 6:5–9)

You will notice, by the way, that the ratio of advice for slaves to advice for owners is four to one.

With regard to the Christian community envisioned by the radical Paul, those texts are contradictory, conservative, and regressive. They are not just post-Pauline; they are anti-Pauline. With regard to the norms of Roman society, they might even be too liberal. First of all, they advocate *reciprocal* duties for slaves and owners—even granted that four-to-one ratio. Second, Paul directly addresses slaves as well as owners, and Roman slave owners would never accept that interference with their property.

THE REACTIONARY PAUL ON SLAVERY

Even the residual vestige of what Roman slave owners might find too liberal rather than appropriately conservative in Colossians and Ephesians is completely eliminated in the letter to Titus:

> Tell slaves to be submissive to their masters and to give satisfaction in every respect; they are not to talk back, not to pilfer, but to show complete and perfect fidelity, so that in everything they may be an ornament to the doctrine of God our Savior. (2:9)

There is nothing there about any mutuality of obligations for slaves and masters. And there is nothing addressed directly to slaves. There is but a single verse, and it begins, "Tell slaves."

SLAVERY AND PATRIARCHY

You can now see clearly—in the test case of slavery—how the radical Paul of the *certainly* Pauline letters is transmuted first into the conservative Paul of the *probably not,* or disputed, Pauline letters and finally into the reactionary Paul of the *certainly not* Pauline letters. How sad, how terribly, terribly sad.

Here is our final question for this chapter. Is the radical Paul's view of slavery along with its deradicalization in the post-Pauline conservative-to-reactionary tradition a unique, special, or individual case? Is the story told in the letter of Philemon simply an isolated, very personal situation between Paul, Philemon, and

Onesimus? Our answer is emphatically negative, because we find exactly that same process with regard to patriarchy. Paul's radicality, in other words, is not simply about slavery or even about patriarchy. It is about Paul's radical repudiation—within Christianity—of the normal hierarchical presuppositions of Roman imperial society.

Watch, therefore, how, as with slavery, the radical Paul is transformed into, first, a conservative and, then, a reactionary pseudo-Paul with regard to patriarchy.

THE RADICAL PAUL
ON PATRIARCHY

Paul's vision of gender equality extends from wife and husband within the Christian family to female and male within the Christian assembly and especially within the Christian apostolate. It involves, in other words, all aspects of Christian life.

Equality in the family. Paul himself was an ascetic celibate and may indeed have already been one in his pre-Christian practice of Judaism—at least he never mentions Jesus as a model for abnegation of that portion of the world's normal social relations. In 1 Corinthians he tells his converts that "I wish that all were as I myself am" (7:7a). Still, he never suggests that every Christian is called to celibacy: "Each has a particular gift from God, one having one kind and another a different kind" (7:7b).

As reason for such celibacy he mentions the "impending crisis," in which "the appointed time has grown short" and "the present form of this world is passing away" (7:26–31). But, once again, he emphasizes that this is personal preference, not apostolic command: "I say this for your own benefit, not to put any restraint upon you, but to promote good order and unhindered devotion to the Lord" (7:35).

Since Paul was wrong about the timing of that consummation, we emphasize that only his vision of special Christian celibacy—never his vision of general Christian life—was derived
from that incorrect presumption. That latter vision involved a
present life *in* Christ regardless of any future action *by* Christ.

The foregoing is but introduction to the important fact that,
throughout all of 1 Corinthians 7, Paul deliberately strains his
syntax to make certain that any obligation of the wife is balanced
by that of the husband and vice versa. It is always about mutual
and reciprocal rights and duties.

In 7:3–4 the subject is abstinence. Paul's sequence of obligations
is: husband/wife and wife/husband (7:3); wife/husband and
husband/wife (7:4). Whatever they decide about abstinence
and intercourse must be "by agreement" (7:5).

In 7:10–16 the subject is divorce. Divorce is not allowed in a
Christian marriage, and the order is again emphatically
mutual: wife/husband and husband/wife (7:10–11). In a
mixed Christian-pagan marriage it may be allowed—if the
pagan party refuses to live at peace (7:15). That applies to
either pagan party—pagan wife of a Christian husband or
pagan husband of a Christian wife (7:12–13). Note, for
example, the reciprocity in these statements: "The unbeliev-
ing husband is made holy through his wife, and the unbe-
lieving wife is made holy through her husband" (7:14); "Wife,
for all you know, you might save your husband. Husband, for
all you know, you might save your wife" (7:16).

In 7:25–28 the subject is virginity. Paul begins with male vir-
gins, asking, "Are you bound to a wife?" (7:25–27), and then
moves to females (7:28).

In 7:29–35 the subject is abstinence—once again. Paul advocates imitation of his own celibate status, since it establishes freedom from the "affairs of the world." That applies, once again, equally to both spouses: "The married man is anxious about the affairs of the world, how to please his wife. . . . The married woman is anxious about the affairs of the world, how to please her husband" (7:32, 34).

It is impossible not to recognize the deliberate balancing of female/male and male/female throughout that chapter. What is right for one is right for the other; what is wrong for one is wrong for the other. Wife and husband are equal in the family.

Equality in the assembly. It is clear, from the opening verses of 1 Corinthians 7, that the Christian equality between husband and wife had created conflict when the wife but not the husband wished to observe that celibacy advocated by Paul. How did equality work in that situation? Paul's advice is: "Do not deprive one another except perhaps by agreement for a set time, to devote yourselves to prayer, and then come together again, so that Satan may not tempt you because of your lack of self-control" (7:5). Good advice, to be sure, but, once again, how would equality work if a wife insisted on her right to celibacy even within marriage?

There is absolutely no scholarly agreement about the problem Paul discusses in 1 Corinthians 11:1–16, but it clearly provoked him to acute rhetorical panic. But what was the problem that generated his very strong, but very strange, reaction? What is at stake when women lead the assembly—but *only* if their hair is veiled?

Our best conjecture—and it can be no more—looks back from 11:1–16 to that preceding 7:1–7. Some married women were insisting on their right to marital celibacy and proclaiming their "virginal" status by removing their married, or matronal, veils. This was creating conflicts not only within the family, but also within the assembly. It was a case where equality and celibacy confronted one another within the marriage contract. Was divorce the only solution?

Paul's argument that married women should be veiled is based on creation (11:8–13) and nature (11:14–15). It even feints toward equality of obligation by adding that "if a man wears long hair, it is degrading to him, but if a woman has long hair, it is her glory." Creation and nature should surely have clinched Paul's argument, but then, as if recognizing its vacuity, he concludes with this anticlimax: "But if anyone is disposed to be contentious—we have no such custom, nor do the churches of God" (11:16). Is Paul's argument based on creation and nature, or mere custom?

In all of this, regardless of what the problem or solution is and regardless of how valid Paul's arguments are, this is most important. From the very start of his discussion, it is explicitly clear that Paul presumes a Christian assembly that includes both "any man who prays or prophesies" and also "any woman who prays or prophesies" (11:4–5). That equality is taken for granted—female and male are equal in the communal Christian assembly just as in the private Christian family.

Equality in the apostolate. The final area of equality is both the most important and the most climactic for Paul. Indeed, if women and men are equal in the Christian apostolate, it is hard to imagine them not already equal in the Christian assembly and the Christian home. Our main evidence is from Romans 16:1–16, and we emphasize how Paul mentions females and males as he greets Christians in Rome whom he knows either personally or at least by name.

First, it is a woman who carries—and therefore reads and explains—Paul's letter from Corinth's eastern port to the Christian groups at Rome. "I commend to you our sister Phoebe, a deacon of the church at Cenchreae, so that you may welcome her in the Lord as is fitting for the saints, and help her in whatever she may require from you, for she has been a benefactor (*prostatis*) of many and of myself as well" (16:1–2). Phoebe is Paul's patron.

Second, two married couples receive extraordinary praise. One is the premier Christian-Gentile couple: "Greet Prisca and Aquila, who work with me in Christ Jesus, and who risked their necks for my life, to whom not only I give thanks, but also all the churches of the Gentiles" (16:3–4). Notice, that Prisc[ill]a is mentioned first in that designation. The other is the premier Christian-Jewish couple: "Greet Andronicus and Junia, my relatives [fellow Jews] who were in prison with me; they are prominent among the apostles, and they were in Christ before I was" (16:7).

Third, of the total of twenty-seven individual Christians in the above list, ten are women (Phoebe, Prisc[ill]a, Mary, Junia, Tryphaena, Tryphosa, Persis, an unnamed mother, Julia, an unnamed sister) and seventeen are men (Aquila, Epaenatus, Andronicus, Ampliatus, Urbanus, Stachys, Apelles, Herodion, Rufus, Asyncritus, Phlegon, Hermes, Patrobas, Hermas, Philologus, Nereus, Olympas). But of those praised, five women (Mary, Tryphaena, Tryphosa, Persis, and that unnamed mother) and six men (Epaenatus, Ampliatus, Urbanus, Stachys, Apelles, Rufus) are singled out for special attention.

Fourth, Paul uses the verb "to work hard" (*kopiaō*) to mean dedicated apostolic activity. He applies it to himself twice, in Galatians 4:11 and 1 Corinthians 15:10. But here he uses it four times and exclusively for women, for Mary (16:6), Tryphaena, Tryphosa, and Persis (16:12).

Finally, we return to that Junia just mentioned (16:7), to a case that would be comic if it were not tragic. For the first millennium of Christianity, commentators recognized correctly that Junia was a female name. She was the wife of Andronicus as Prisc[ill]a was the wife of Aquila. Then, for the second millennium of Christianity, she was turned into a male. Junia, so the claim went, was short for the male name Junianus. That, however, was patently untrue because, although there were over 250 known cases of a female Junia in antiquity, there was not a single one of a male Junia as the abbreviation of Junianus.

The reason for that rather desperate claim was also quite clear. If Junia were allowed to remain a female, then, since she was "prominent among the apostles," it was obviously possible for a woman to be an apostle. Paul, of course, had no problem with that combination of gender and function. For him women as well as men were called by God to be apostles of Christ. The Christian gender equality that existed in marriage and home also prevailed in assembly and apostolate.

THE CONSERVATIVE PAUL
ON PATRIARCHY

We are back once more with the ethics for extended families seen above with regard to slavery. Read with us through these full household codes for specifically Christian homes. As you do so, notice their multiple layers of hierarchy. Vertically from top to bottom the order is descending, from parents to children to slaves. Horizontally within each set the order is from inferior to superior: first wives, then husbands; first children, then fathers; first slaves, then masters:

wives and husbands	Colossians 3:18, 19	Ephesians 5:22–24, 25–33
children and fathers	Colossians 3:20, 21	Ephesians 6:1–3, 4
slaves and masters	Colossians 3:22–25; 4:1	Ephesians 6:5–8, 9

You will also notice that, internally, it is not a matter of children and *parents,* but of children and *fathers,* and not of slaves and *owners,* but of slaves and *masters.*

Actually, as we saw above in Roman attitudes toward slaves, a Roman *paterfamilias,* or father of the household, would probably consider the above admonitions far too liberal. First of all, they require mutual and reciprocal, even if unequal and hierarchical, obligations. Second, those deemed inferiors—wives, children, slaves—are addressed directly and not through their presumed superiors—husbands, fathers, masters.

Be that as it may, we focus here on wives and husbands to emphasize how, in those two texts, Pauline Christian gender equality is deradicalized back into Roman gender hierarchy:

> *Wives,* be subject to your husbands, as is fitting in the Lord. (Col. 3:18)

> *Husbands,* love your wives and never treat them harshly. (Col. 3:19)

> *Wives,* be subject to your husbands as you are to the Lord. For the husband is the head of the wife just as Christ is the head of the church, the body of which he is the Savior. Just as the church is subject to Christ, so also wives ought to be, in everything, to their husbands. (Eph. 5:22–24)

> *Husbands,* love your wives, just as Christ loved the church and gave himself up for her, in order to make her holy by cleansing her with the washing of water by the word, so as to present the church to himself in splendor, without a spot or wrinkle or anything of the kind—yes, so that she may be holy and without blemish. In the same way, husbands should love their wives as they do their own

bodies. He who loves his wife loves himself. For no one ever hates his own body, but he nourishes and tenderly cares for it, just as Christ does for the church, because we are members of his body. "For this reason a man will leave his father and mother and be joined to his wife, and the two will become one flesh." This is a great mystery, and I am applying it to Christ and the church. Each of you, however, should love his wife as himself, and a wife should respect her husband. (Eph. 5:25–33)

You will notice that wives and husbands get one verse each in Colossians, but in Ephesians the ratio is three to nine. That would indicate that husbands are the greater problem in the second of those two pseudo-Pauline letters. Furthermore, Ephesians places a far heavier burden on husbands than on wives. For wives to obey their husbands as the church does Christ is surely easier than for husbands to sacrifice themselves for their wives as Christ did for the church. That latter injunction probably means that, if there is a religious persecution, husbands must be ready to die if that would save their wives. It is surely sad that subsequent Christian tradition demanded subjection from wives and then, rather than demanding self-sacrifice from husbands, transferred that to wives as well.

THE REACTIONARY PAUL
ON PATRIARCHY

In what scholars call the pastoral letters, Timothy and Titus are imagined as left by Paul in charge of Ephesus and Crete, respectively. The subject of female leadership within the Christian assembly arises in a letter of pseudo-Paul to Timothy, and in this (in)famous text it is absolutely forbidden:

> Let a woman learn in silence with full submission. I per-
> mit no woman to teach or to have authority over a man;
> she is to keep silent. For Adam was formed first, then
> Eve; and Adam was not deceived, but the woman was
> deceived and became a transgressor. Yet she will be saved
> through childbearing, provided they continue in faith
> and love and holiness, with modesty. (1 Tim. 2:11–15)

We call this passage "reactionary" and not just "conservative,"
because it is clearly reacting to what has been happening. There
would be no reason to forbid what nobody had ever imagined.
There is, for example, no Roman decree forbidding female sena-
tors, because nobody ever imagined that possibility, let alone
practiced it.

There is, however, one other text on the subject of female
leadership from an authentic Pauline letter that requires careful discussion, lest our claims about it seem like special plead-
ing. Scholars have suggested that certain units within the seven
original Pauline letters were inserted at a later date. But this is
only considered persuasive within scholarship if certain criteria
are met. Here are the main ones. First, the text before and after
it should read as well or better with the alleged insert removed.
Second, there should be objective evidence of problems with its
presence within the manuscript tradition. Finally, it should con-
tradict other authentic texts from the author. And those three
criteria are present for 1 Corinthians 14:33b–36:

> (As in all the churches of the saints, women should be si-
> lent in the churches. For they are not permitted to speak,
> but should be subordinate, as the law also says. If there
> is anything they desire to know, let them ask their hus-
> bands at home. For it is shameful for a woman to speak
> in church. Or did the word of God originate with you?
> Or are you the only ones it has reached?)

First, the subject of the text before this passage, 14:26–33a, is *prophecy*, and that same subject is continued in 14:37–40 after it. In other words, if you remove 14:33b–36, the continuity is better than with it.

Second, that disputed section is not given after 14:33a, but at the end of the chapter, after 14:40, in some early manuscripts. Furthermore, those verses are given as a separate paragraph in all Greek manuscripts. It is also like that in our modern, official Greek New Testament. That is why the New Revised Standard Version, given above, puts that entire unit in a separate paragraph and in parentheses.

Finally, this silencing of women in church not only contradicts the general attitude of the radical Paul just seen above, but it explicitly contradicts what he said earlier in 1 Corinthians. He insists there that, in the Christian assembly, "any man who prays or prophesies with something on his head disgraces his head, but any woman who prays or prophesies with her head unveiled disgraces her head" (11:4–5). Whatever the problem is with veils at Corinth, it is clear that both men and women minister publicly in the Christian assembly.

All in all, therefore, the best explanation for 14:33b–36 is that a scribe had just copied out 14:33a, which states, "God is a God not of disorder but of peace," and, considering female teachers an example of such disorder, added this summary of 1 Timothy 2:8–15 in the margin of the manuscript at this point. Thence it was later inserted into the text at different places—after 14:33a or 14:40 by subsequent copyists.

THE DERADICALIZATION OF PAUL

We conclude this chapter by reminding you of the implications of deradicalization. We looked at two cases—slavery and patriarchy—and saw exactly the same process at work:

	Radical Paul	Conservative "Paul"	Reactionary "Paul"
Slavery	*Philemon*	Col. 3:22–4:1; Eph. 6:5–9	Titus 2:9
Patriarchy	1 Cor. 7; Rom. 16	Col. 3:18–19; Eph. 5:22–33	1 Tim. 2:8–15; 1 Cor. 14:33b–36

It is that similarity and symmetry that convince us of the overall and deliberate deradicalization of Paul as we move from the authentic through the disputed to the inauthentic letters, as we move, in other words, from the radical and historical Paul to the conservative and reactionary pseudo-Paul or even anti-Paul.

That, of course, opens up a series of questions for future consideration. Where did Paul get that vision of Christian equality? In what is it grounded and how does it connect with God and Christ? We hold those very basic questions until Chapter 4, after we consider, in Chapter 3, the life of Paul.

CHAPTER THREE

THE LIFE OF
A LONG-DISTANCE
APOSTLE

To reconstruct the historical Jesus, you must make a careful comparison and delicate assessment of four main New Testament sources—Matthew, Mark, Luke, and John. To reconstruct the historical Paul, you must do the same for two main New Testament sources—Paul's own letters and Luke's Acts of the Apostles. And for Paul, as for Jesus, you must always recognize differences within those sources, differences in authorial intentions and historical situations. In this chapter, therefore, watch where Paul and Luke agree or disagree, and especially where they agree on the information, but disagree on its interpretation.

TARSUS

In Acts, Paul says in Greek to a Roman officer in Jerusalem, "I am a Jew, from Tarsus in Cilicia, a citizen of an important city" (21:39). Immediately he repeats that same natal claim to a wider Jewish audience in Aramaic: "I am a Jew, born in Tarsus in Cilicia" (22:3).

In the first century, Tarsus was the capital city of the Roman province of Cilicia and the dominant city of the fertile plain that surrounded it. Thirty miles to its north were the cold peaks of the Taurus Mountains, and ten miles to its south were the warm waters of the Mediterranean coast. Today, Adana on the Seyhan River has far outstripped Tarsus on the Cydnus River as the dominant city of the agriculturally fertile Çukurova Plain, but at the time of Paul's birth Tarsus, not Adana, was queen of Cilicia. And Tarsus on the Cydnus was a birthplace both fortunate and unfortunate for Paul as an itinerant apostle of Jesus.

Paul was born around 8 CE, and his birth at Tarsus gave him three very good gifts and one rather bad one—although he himself would have disagreed with that last designation. And all of those gifts, good or bad, helpful or unhelpful, came from the same urban feature: location, location, location.

The first positive gift was *vista* and involved the advantages of a frontier city between the Greek and the Semitic worlds. We think today of the Mediterranean fault line between West and East as extending along the Dardanelles to the Bosphorus and splitting the modern city of Istanbul into European and Asian sections. At the turn of the era, you could more easily imagine it as extending along the Cydnus River and splitting into two parts, as it were, the ancient city of Tarsus.

Tarsus looked toward both the West and the East. Those born there could easily imagine going north through the Cilician Gates in the Taurus Mountains and then west toward Asia Minor and Greece. They could just as easily imagine going east through the Syrian Gates in the Amanus Mountains and then south toward Israel and Egypt. Tarsus gave Paul an early vision of sea and mountain, gorge and river, gave him an early vista of difficult actualities, but open possibilities.

The second positive gift was *labor* and involved an appreciation for what could be accomplished by hard work. The Tarsians made their city even as their city made them. To the south and the Mediterranean Sea, they had engineered a secure harbor from their river's gift of a large lagoon. To the north and the Anatolian plateau, they had engineered a wagon road through their mountain's gift of a deep defile. Tarsians connected together the open vista of the Mediterranean Sea, the steamy marsh of the Cilician plain, the icy cold of the Taurus range, and the baked heat of the Anatolian plateau. Geography was destiny, to be sure, but hard work could change geography and thus change history as well.

The third positive gift was *education* and involved Jewish synagogue teaching in a Greek university city. In Strabo's *Geography*, written when Paul was a young man, Tarsus's university status gets very high marks. It "surpassed Athens, Alexandria, or any other place that can be named where there have been schools and lectures of philosophers." It also had "all kinds of schools of rhetoric," and, indeed, "it is Rome that is best able to tell us the number of learned men from that city; for it is full of Tarsians and Alexandrians" (14.5).

Athens and Alexandria might have scoffed at that comparison but, if so, they would have done it quietly. After all, it was a Tarsian philosopher named Athenodorus who was teaching the nineteen-year-old Octavian at Apollonia in northwestern Greece, when his pupil's great-uncle Julius Caesar was assassinated in 44 BCE. Athenodorus immediately accompanied Octavian back to Rome and stayed with him for the next thirty years, as that student became the divine Augustus, emperor of the Roman world.

Athenodorus finally returned home to Tarsus about a dozen years before Paul was born and, as its university's principal, proceeded successfully to reform that city's constitution and lead its government. William Mitchell Ramsay, the first professor of classical archaeology at Oxford, concluded in his *The Cities of St. Paul* that "Tarsus in the reign of Augustus is the one example known in history of a State ruled by a University through its successive principals."[1]

In that environment a smart boy like Paul would have received not only a specific education in his own Jewish tradition, but also some general knowledge of the Greek philosophical schools and Greek rhetorical strategies. And, especially in that contentious environment, he would have been schooled in apologetics for internal and polemics for external usage. It was an education magnificently suited for a permanently away-from-home apostle who had learned to carry scripture in memory, to interweave citation with citation, and to argue orally on his feet as well as propose an argument as text.

The major negative gift of Tarsus was malaria, but that conclusion moves within the higher reaches of scholarship known as—conjecture. Think for a moment, however, about that Cilician plain locked between the mountains and the sea. Think of its rich fertility and agricultural prosperity fed by three rivers that annually drained the melting snows of the Taurus range. Despite the best Roman drainage engineering, that environment also meant marshes, mosquitoes, and *malaria*.

Paul's first stay in the newly created Roman province of Galatia was not part of any planned program of missionary activity because, as he reminded the Galatians in a later and rather fiercely pugnacious letter:

> You know that it was because of a physical infirmity [in Greek, *weakness* of the *flesh*] that I first announced the gospel to you; though my condition put you to the test, you

did not scorn or despise me, but welcomed me as an angel of God, as Christ Jesus. What has become of the goodwill you felt? For I testify that, had it been possible, you would have torn out your eyes and given them to me. (4:13–15)

Was Paul's "physical infirmity" an isolated incident or was it part of the wider "thorn in the *flesh*" mentioned in 2 Corinthians 12:7?

First, "thorn" (Greek *skolops*) means more than a minor pinprick. It is, as a standard Greek lexicon explains, "'something pointed' such as a '(pointed) stake,' then something that causes serious annoyances, thorn, splinter, etc., specifically of an injurious foreign body."

Second, Paul makes a connection between his ecstatic (literally, "standing out of the body") experiences and that "thorn/stake in the flesh." He begins by describing "visions and revelations of the Lord" when he was "caught up to the third heaven—whether in the body or out of the body" and was permitted to hear "things that are not to be told, that no mortal is permitted to repeat" (12:1–3). He continues:

> Therefore, to keep me from being too elated, a thorn was given me in the *flesh,* a messenger of Satan to torment me, to keep me from being too elated. Three times I appealed to the Lord about this, that it would leave me, but he said to me, "My grace is sufficient for you, for power is made perfect in *weakness.*" (12:7–9)

We italicized "weakness" and "flesh" there in 2 Corinthians 12:7–9 to link it with those same words italicized above in Galatians 4:13. We think, therefore, that Paul had some recurrent illness that may have precipitated or accompanied ecstatic experience. But what was that humbling illness?

Our answer depends on another, earlier book by William Mitchell Ramsay, his *St. Paul the Traveler and the Roman Citizen*. He combined Galatians 4:13 with 2 Corinthians 12:7 and proposed that Paul's recurring illness "was a species of chronic malaria fever," which

> tends to recur in very distressing and prostrating paroxysms, whenever one's energies are taxed for a great effort. Such an attack is for the time absolutely incapacitating: the sufferer can only lie and feel himself a shaking and helpless weakling, when he ought to be at work. He feels a contempt and loathing for self, and believes that others feel equal contempt and loathing.[2]

He adds, as collaborating evidence for his diagnosis, that Paul's phrase "a stake in the flesh"—that is his translation of *skolops*—"is the peculiar headache which accompanies the paroxysms [of chronic malarial fever]: within my experience several persons, innocent of Pauline theorizing, have described it as 'like a red-hot bar thrust through the forehead.'"[3]

We propose, following Ramsay, that Paul had contracted malaria during his youth at Tarsus from a climate that easily produced the chills and fevers, the uncontrollable shivering and profuse sweating, the severe headache, nausea, and vomiting of chronic malarial fever. The "thorn *or* stake in the flesh" may have been Tarsus's most permanent mark on Paul.

Only Luke's Acts gives us that important information about Tarsus as Paul's birthplace. But the Luke of the two-volume work that tradition calls the Gospel According to Luke and the Acts of the Apostles is not the same "Luke" mentioned by Paul in Philemon 24 or by post-Pauline writers in Colossians 4:14 ("the beloved physician") and 2 Timothy 4:11. Furthermore, there is no persuasive evidence that this Luke of the two-volume gospel knows any of the Pauline letters—or, if he does, that he agrees with their theology. This Luke is writing two generations after Paul, at a different time and place, for a different audience and situation, with a different purpose and intention; although he knows exactly what *he* intends to do at the end of the first century, it is not what *Paul* intended to do in its middle.

But, in any case, in spite of the fact that only Luke records that Paul's life began in Tarsus, both Luke and Paul emphasize how it was changed forever by a transformative vision of Christ at Damascus, that great and ancient city brought under Roman control by Pompey in the first century BCE. But before that climactic moment, what else do we know about Paul's biographical identity?

BETWEEN TARSUS AND DAMASCUS

First, with regard to religious and educational status, Paul and Luke agree that Paul was a fervent Pharisaic Jew. That may seem obvious, but some of his fellow Jews and fellow Christians—then and now—judged Paul an apostate from both Judaism and Christianity. But in his own mind, heart, and conscience, he lived and died as a Jew—a Messianic or Christian Jew, to be sure—but with both adjective and noun inextricably interlinked. Listen to his own words:

> I myself am an Israelite, a descendant of Abraham, a member of the tribe of Benjamin. (Rom. 11:1)

> Are they Hebrews? So am I. Are they Israelites? So am I. Are they descendants of Abraham? So am I. (2 Cor. 11:22)

> I advanced in Judaism beyond many among my people of the same age, for I was far more zealous for the traditions of my ancestors. (Gal. 1:14)

> Circumcised on the eighth day, a member of the people of Israel, of the tribe of Benjamin, a Hebrew born of Hebrews; as to the law, a Pharisee; . . . as to righteousness under the law, blameless. (Phil. 3:5–6)

Also, in 2 Corinthians 11:26 Paul lists the dangers he has faced, one of which is "danger from my own people (*genous*)." Notice that the danger is not from "Jews," but from "my own people."

Luke's Acts has similar information, but it is given there as autobiographical information on Paul's own lips:

> I am a Jew, from Tarsus in Cilicia, a citizen of an important city. (21:39)

> I am a Jew, born in Tarsus in Cilicia, but brought up in this city [Jerusalem] at the feet of Gamaliel, educated strictly according to our ancestral law, being zealous for God, just as all of you are today. (22:3)

> I am a Pharisee, a son of Pharisees. (23:6)

> I have belonged to the strictest sect of our religion and lived as a Pharisee. (26:5)

To understand the term "Pharisees" you must ignore the bitter polemical (because closely intrafamilial?) attacks against them in the gospels. Think, instead, of their purity laws as the visible and sacramental signs of invisible and spiritual sanctity, of being, as the Lukan Paul says, "zealous for God."

We also think that Luke is probably upgrading rather than just describing Paul's religio-educational status by naming him not only "a Pharisee," but a "son of Pharisees," and having him "brought up in this city [Jerusalem] at the feet of Gamaliel." It seems much more likely that Paul received his higher religious education at Damascus rather than Jerusalem. But in any case, if Gamaliel were his teacher at Jerusalem, Paul did not follow his master's advice on how to handle dissident Christian Jews. Gamaliel proposed to "keep away from these men and let them alone" (Acts 5:38), but Paul, as we see below, persecuted them.

Second, with regard to socioeconomic status, Luke insists that Paul was a Roman citizen, but Paul himself never mentions that status and seems even to negate it. When Luke describes Paul's arrest in Jerusalem, for example, he repeatedly mentions the term "Roman citizen" by creating dialogue about it. Here is the full text:

> When they had tied him up with thongs, Paul said to the centurion who was standing by, "Is it legal for you to flog a *Roman citizen* who is uncondemned?" When the centurion heard that, he went to the tribune and said to him, "What are you about to do? This man is a *Roman citizen*." The tribune came and asked Paul, "Tell me, are you a *Roman citizen*?" And he said, "Yes." The tribune answered, "It cost me a large sum of money to get my citizenship." Paul said, "But I was born a *citizen*." Immediately those who were about to examine him drew back from him; and the tribune also was afraid, for he realized that Paul was a *Roman citizen* and that he had bound him. . . . This man [the tribune reported later] was seized by the Jews and was about to be killed by them, but when I had learned that he was a *Roman citizen,* I came with the guard and rescued him. (Acts 22:25–29; 23:27)

But what do we learn from Paul about that alleged status? Does he ever say anything or act, directly or indirectly, to indicate such a status?

On the one hand, it would have been very easy for Paul to have been a Roman citizen. Were his father a slave freed by a

Roman citizen, his father would have then become a freed Roman citizen himself, and if Paul were born after that liberation, he would have been a freeborn Roman citizen. So Luke's claim is not at all impossible.

On the other hand, Paul himself never makes a single reference to that status and admits, in fact, that "three times I was beaten with rods" (2 Cor. 11:25)—a Roman punishment forbidden to be used on Roman citizens. Indeed, Luke himself seems to have forgotten that when he has Paul and Silas "beaten with rods" (Acts 16:22). All in all, therefore, Paul was either not a Roman citizen or, if he were, he never used that privilege for his own advantage. And, indeed, that abstention could be the far more important point.

Finally, we move beyond Paul's general religio-educational and socioeconomic status to a very personal and individual identity—that of the pre-Christian Jewish Paul as a persecutor of Christian Jews. And here, once again, Luke and Paul are in explicit agreement:

> I was violently persecuting the church of God and was trying to destroy it. (Gal. 1:13–14)

> As to zeal, a persecutor of the church. (Phil. 3:6)

> I am the least of the apostles, unfit to be called an apostle, because I persecuted the church of God. (1 Cor. 15:9)

> Being zealous for God. . . . I persecuted this Way up to the point of death by binding both men and women and putting them in prison. (Acts 22:3–4)

But of course, for Luke, Paul was almost a persecutor even in Jerusalem (Acts 7:58; 8:1), although Paul himself says that he was "still unknown by sight to the churches of Judea that are in Christ" (Gal. 1:22).

Notice also that both Paul and Luke use that term "zeal(ous)," and in Jewish religious contexts that often denotes paralegal and even lethal action against those considered apostates. We are dealing not just with discrimination, but with very serious and even mortal persecution.

What, by the way, was so wrong with Christian Judaism—or at least the part that concerned Paul—that made him launch a lethal persecution against it? We can only conjecture, but here is our best reconstruction. Some Christian Jews claimed that the awaited eschatological era was already present, that, in other words, the kingdom of God's divine transformation of the world from one of violent injustice to one of nonviolent justice had already begun. Therefore, they concluded, Gentiles could now become full members of the people of God without following Jewish conversion requirements, for example, circumcision for males. Paul began as an opponent of this belief, but was converted to being a proponent of exactly the same belief—he went from persecuting those proposing open Gentile inclusion to becoming its major missionary advocate.

DESTINY AT DAMASCUS

We turn now to focus on Damascus. Both Luke and Paul connect that city to the inaugural event of Paul's vocational revelation from God and Christ. But they do it quite differently when describing its two elements—Paul's vision of Christ and Paul's mandate as an apostle. And in both those areas the differences are major theological and not just minor historical ones.

A vision of Christ. Luke's account is the famous "on the road to Damascus" story, which he records three times to emphasize its importance in Acts: first, as it happens (9:1–19); then, as Paul tells it to the Roman officer in Jerusalem (22:3–21); and, finally, as Paul tells it to the Jewish king, Agrippa II, at Caesarea Maritima (26:1–18).

There are two major problems with Luke's version of that event. First, Luke claims that Paul's vocational revelation occurred as he traveled from Jerusalem to Damascus with high-priestly authority to bring back dissident Jewish Christians for punishment (9:1–2; 22:4–5; 26:9–12). That is quite impossible, since the Jerusalem high priests lacked any power to dispense capital punishment or exercise trans-border authority. It is simply part of Luke's emphasis on Jewish responsibility for opposition to Christianity, on everything starting out from Jerusalem, and maybe even on upgrading Paul's résumé—even as a persecutor, he was an authoritative superpersecutor. Unfortunately, therefore, that Lukan location *"on the road to* Damascus" with high-priestly authority for punitive rendition is fiction—as is the horse seen with Paul in medieval paintings of that scene.

Second, Luke's well-known scenario emphasizes that what Paul *saw* was a light from heaven and what Paul *heard* was the voice of Christ:

> A light from heaven flashed around him. He fell to the ground and heard a voice. (9:3–4)

> "A great light from heaven suddenly shone about me. I fell to the ground and heard a voice." (22:6–7)

> "I saw a light from heaven, brighter than the sun, shining around me and my companions. When we had all fallen to the ground, I heard a voice." (26:13–14)

In other words, for Luke in Acts, and with a threefold repetition, Paul saw the light, not the Lord, and heard only the voice of

Christ, but never saw his face. But what does Paul himself tell us about that inaugural revelation at Damascus?

Paul's own account of his inaugural revelation also mentions—but quite indirectly—the city of Damascus:

> The gospel that was proclaimed by me . . . I received it through a revelation of Jesus Christ. . . . I was violently persecuting the church of God and was trying to destroy it. . . . But when God . . . was pleased to reveal his Son to me, so that I might proclaim him among the Gentiles, . . . I went away at once into Arabia, and afterwards I returned to Damascus. (Gal. 1:11–17)

He presumes his audience knows that the story started in Damascus, so that "returned to" makes sense to them. In other words, he was living in Damascus and persecuting Jewish Christians there—most likely within its synagogue. There is nothing, of course, about high-priestly authorized travels to Damascus with the right of rendition back to Jerusalem. But this next difference is much more important.

Luke says Paul only *heard* Christ, but Paul insists he *saw* Christ. Indeed, it is the *sight* of Christ that makes him an apostle, as he says in 1 Corinthians: "Am I not an apostle? Have I not seen Jesus our Lord?" (9:1). It is that *sight* that puts him on a par with the Twelve and all the other earlier apostles: "Last of all, as to one untimely born, he appeared [Greek *ophthē*, 'was seen'] also to me. For I am the least of the apostles, unfit to be called an apostle, because I persecuted the church of God" (15:8–9).

Paul already knew enough about the life, death, and resurrection of Jesus to persecute his followers for proclaiming their faith to fellow Jews at Damascus. In Christian gospel, art, and mysticism, the risen Christ retains the wounds of historical crucifixion even on his glorified and transcendental body. Those wounds do not heal or fade. They are forever there. To take seriously Paul's claim to have *seen* the risen Jesus, we suggest that his inaugural vision was of Jesus's body simultaneously crucified (by Rome) *and* glorified (by God). Such a stunning vocational vision would already contain foundationally the full message of Paul's faith and theology, the full meaning of Paul's life and death.

An apostle of Christ. That preceding divergence between Paul and Luke leads directly into a second major disagreement between them, and it too concerns much more than autobiographical details and résumé upgrades. It involves Paul's very identity, integrity, and authority as a Christian apostle.

An "apostle" is a person "sent" somewhere (from Greek *apostellein*, "to send") in order to found new Christian communities. But by whom is an apostle "sent"? According to Paul, he is an apostle called and sent directly by Christ—just as were the Twelve—but according to Luke Paul has no such status or authority. He is only an apostle sent by the community at Antioch and is therefore subordinate to Antioch, and through Antioch to Jerusalem and the Twelve.

As you can understand, there are profound theological implications to that difference. Do God and Christ call an apostle by revelatory vocation (from Latin *vocare*, "to call") directly from heaven even after the resurrection and ascension, or only indirectly through the Christian community here below?

So for Luke in Acts, Paul is an apostle sent by Jerusalem and Antioch. Here is how Paul becomes an "apostle" according to Luke in Acts 13:1–3, but notice that Barnabas is mentioned first and seems much more important than Saul/Paul in this account:

> In the church at Antioch there were prophets and teachers: Barnabas, Simeon who was called Niger, Lucius of Cyrene, Manaen a member of the court of Herod

the ruler, and Saul. While they were worshiping the Lord and fasting, the Holy Spirit said, "Set apart for me Barnabas and Saul for the work to which I have called them." Then after fasting and praying they laid their hands on them and sent them off (*apelusan*).

For Luke, Paul is an "apostle" sent by God, but only indirectly through the Antioch community as it prays and worships in the Holy Spirit. And, indeed, the Greek verb for "sent" in that Acts 13:3 is not the solemn and official *apostellein* (whence our term "apostle"). Still, after that introduction, Luke calls Barnabas and Paul "apostles" in a few cases, for example, at Iconium and Lystra on that same mission in Acts 14:4, 14.

For the most part, however, the special term "apostles" is reserved by Luke for the Twelve. Jesus "called his disciples and chose twelve of them, whom he also named apostles" (Luke 6:13). Then, as Acts opens, Peter announces that a replacement must be found for Judas, who betrayed Jesus, so that the full number of the twelve apostles will be preserved:

> One of the men [*andres*, males] who have accompanied us during all the time that the Lord Jesus went in and out among us, beginning from the baptism of John until the day when he was taken up from us—one of these must become a witness with us to his resurrection. . . . And they cast lots for them, and the lot fell on Matthias; and he was added to the eleven apostles. (Acts 1:21–22, 26)

Thereafter, throughout Acts, when Luke refers to "the apostles" he means "the twelve apostles" named in 1:13, 26. They are a closed male group called by Jesus at the start of his public life, and into that group Paul could never enter. For Luke, Paul is emphatically not an apostle sent by any personal revelation made directly to him by God or Christ.

Paul, however, believes himself to be an apostle sent by God and Christ. For example, in the greeting that opens several of his letters, Paul identifies himself explicitly and immediately as an apostle:

> Paul, a servant of Jesus Christ, called to be an apostle, set apart for the gospel of God. (Rom. 1:1)

> Paul, called to be an apostle of Christ Jesus by the will of God. (1 Cor. 1:1)

> Paul, an apostle of Christ Jesus by the will of God. (2 Cor. 1:1)

> Paul an apostle—sent neither by human commission nor from human authorities, but through Jesus Christ and God the Father, who raised him from the dead. (Gal. 1:1)

That final greeting comes from a situation where it is precisely his direct heavenly mandate and therefore his full apostolic authority that have been questioned.

Furthermore, Paul explicitly insists that his own apostolic authority is just as valid as that of the Twelve and that, besides them, there are many more apostles—including himself:

> Christ appeared to Cephas, then to the twelve. Then he appeared to more than five hundred brothers and sisters at one time, most of whom are still alive, though some have died. Then he appeared to James, then to all the apostles. Last of all, as to one untimely born, he appeared also to me. For I am the least of the apostles,

unfit to be called an apostle, because I persecuted the church of God. (1 Cor. 15:5–9)

But, of course, if you are "the least of the apostles," you are still an apostle. And this disagreement over Paul's apostolic identity derives ultimately from the very different accounts of that inaugural Damascus revelation.

THE NABATEAN MISSION

Paul told the Galatians that, immediately after his vocational revelation from God and his ecstatic encounter with Christ: "I did not go up to Jerusalem to those who were already apostles before me, but I went away at once into Arabia, and afterwards I returned to Damascus. Then after three years I did go up to Jerusalem" (1:17–18). What did Paul do in Arabia for three years?

Some scholars suggest that he went to the desert to meditate on and prepare for his missionary vocation. But no prophet acted like that—and certainly not one like Paul. He was called by God and Christ to do something—not to think about doing something. We propose, therefore, that "into Arabia" meant Paul's immediate obedience to his vocation as Apostle of the Gentiles. It involved, in other words, his first mission—to the Nabatean Arabs, whose capital was at Petra in modern Jordan.

Paul passes over this first mission in silence, and Luke never mentions it at all. But as we shall see below, both of them record Paul's ignominious departure from Damascus at its conclusion. Why was this mission such a disaster? It had nothing to do with theological debates over male circumcision, for example, since Nabatean males were already circumcised. It had to do with very unfortunate timing for a Jewish preacher among Arab listeners.

At the end of the 20s, Herod Antipas, tetrarch of Galilee and Perea, divorced his wife, who was the daughter of Aretas IV, king of the Nabateans, in order to marry the Hasmonean princess Herodias. Aretas, as the insulted father-in-law, first bided his time, then went to war against Antipas in 36 CE and soundly defeated him. Aretas was only saved from severe Roman punishment for disturbing the peace by the death of the emperor Tiberius in March of 37 CE.

In other words, at the very time that the Jewish Paul was conducting a mission to convert the Nabateans to Christian Judaism, their king was conducting a war to defeat the Jewish tetrarch Herod Antipas. When, therefore, Aretas acquired Damascus between 37 and 39 CE, Paul's base for Arabia was now under his control and Paul's days there were numbered.

Paul's first mission to the Nabatean Gentiles left no traces in our extant texts save, of course, for those Lukan and Pauline versions of his escape from a Damascus controlled by Aretas. We ask you to compare the following two escape accounts very carefully, because they are an absolutely classic example of Paul and Luke having exactly the same information, but very different interpretations. Luke's version is first, followed by Paul's:

> After some time had passed, the Jews plotted to kill him, but their plot became known to Saul. They were watching the gates day and night so that they might kill him; but his disciples took him by night and let him down through an opening in the wall, lowering him in a basket. (Acts 9:23–25)

> In Damascus, the governor under King Aretas guarded the city of Damascus in order to seize me, but I was let down in a basket through a window in the wall, and escaped from his hands. (2 Cor. 11:32–33)

In Paul's version the threat comes—very credibly—from the Nabatean *civil* authorities, who controlled the gates of Arab Damascus after 37 CE. For Luke it comes—quite incredibly—from the Jewish *religious* authorities, who never could have controlled the gates of Arab Damascus. This reveals a Lukan interpretive prejudice that must be carefully assessed throughout Acts for its anti-Judaism. Notice also, by the way, that the problem is civil and political for Paul, but religious and theological for Luke.

THE CYPRO-GALATIAN MISSION

After that first failed mission, "I went," Paul told the Galatians, "into the regions of Syria and Cilicia" (1:21). Paul may well have been crushed by that inaugural failure and stumbled home to recover. Notice, for example, how those geographical locations are repeated in Luke's comment in Acts 11:25–26 that, "Barnabas went to Tarsus [Cilicia] to look for Saul, and when he had found him, he brought him to Antioch [Syria]." And so began Paul's second mission—to Cyprus and Galatia—but *with* and *under* Barnabas.

Paul never tells us anything directly about this second mission, but Luke gives it in very full detail in Acts 13–14. We already saw above that it opened at Antioch with Paul clearly subordinate to Barnabas. Notice this sequence: "In the church at Antioch there were prophets and teachers: Barnabas, Simeon, . . . Lucius, . . . Manaen, . . . and Saul" (13:1). And again: "'Set apart for me Barnabas and Saul for the work to which I have called them'" (13:2). Later, on that same mission, Paul healed a cripple and, "when the crowds saw what Paul had done, they shouted in the Lycaonian language, 'The gods have come down to us in human form!' Barnabas they called Zeus, and Paul they called Hermes, because he was the chief speaker" (14:11–12). Hermes, of course, is subordinate to Zeus as, on this mission, Paul is to Barnabas.

If you study the itinerary in Acts 13–14, you can see Barnabas's missionary strategy and understand how it differs from Paul's on Paul's third and final mission. Barnabas's method was city hopping along major Roman roads. They sailed from Syrian Antioch's port of Seleucia to Cyprus and then went from east to west across that island. Then they sailed to southern Galatia and traveled through Perga, Pisidian Antioch, Iconium, and Lystra to Derbe. From Derbe they reversed that journey and sailed home—bypassing Cyprus—to Syrian Antioch.

Luke clearly knows their route and gives accurately the older, pre-Roman regional names such as Pamphylia, Pisidia, and Lycaonia. Barnabas, says Luke, goes to the synagogues in each city and attempts to convert Jews to the messianic Jesus, but has greater success with Gentiles. Paul watched, Paul learned, and Paul changed. It is not even certain that Paul returned to Syrian Antioch with Barnabas. He may have left him at Derbe and headed northward onto the arid Anatolian plateau. Possibly the moist Pamphylian climate had resulted in malarial relapses because, as we saw above, he later reminded the Galatians, "It was because of a physical infirmity that I first announced the gospel to you" (4:13).

Be that as it may, we can now see why Luke's Acts always has Paul going into synagogues to convert the Jews. Luke had special traditions about Barnabas in the first half of Acts. He introduces him as "a Levite, a native of Cyprus, Joseph, to whom the apostles gave the name Barnabas (which means 'son of encouragement'). He sold a field that belonged to him, then brought the money, and laid it at the apostles' feet" (4:36–37). He has Barnabas vouch for Paul at Jerusalem after his conversion: "Barnabas took him [Paul], brought him to the apostles, and described for them how on the road he had seen the Lord, who had spoken to him, and how in Damascus he had spoken boldly in the name of Jesus" (9:27). And, as just noted, he has Barnabas bring Paul back from his Tarsus refuge after that failed Nabatean mission (11:25). Finally, Luke has famine relief sent from Antioch to Jerusalem "by Barnabas and Saul" (11:30).

In other words, Luke takes Barnabas's mission—and what Paul did when he was under Barnabas—as a model for what Paul always did even when he was by himself. Luke filled out his lesser knowledge of Paul on his own with his greater knowledge of Paul under Barnabas. But is that what Paul did when he was on his own independent mission? And, first of all, how did he finally gain that independence?

THE AEGEAN MISSION

At the end of Paul's second mission—that one under Barnabas in the 40s—there was a major apostolic agreement in Jerusalem and a major apostolic disagreement at Antioch. Paul details the former event in Galatians 2:1–10 and the latter in 2:11–14, but Luke speaks only of agreement at both Jerusalem and Antioch in Acts 15.

The debate at Jerusalem was whether gentile males who converted to Christianity had to be circumcised. And, as Paul reminded the Galatians, "James and Cephas and John, who were acknowledged pillars, . . . gave to Barnabas and me the right hand of fellowship, agreeing that we should go to the Gentiles and they to the circumcised" (2:9). That was a crucial apostolic agreement for Paul. Simon, by the way, had a bilingual nickname, Cephas in Aramaic and Peter in Greek. Both terms meant "the Rock" or, if you prefer, Rocky.

The debate at Antioch was whether a mixed community of Jewish and gentile Christians should observe kosher rules in their common eucharistic meals. Should it be *kosher for all,* with the gentile Christians deferring to the Jewish Christians? Or should it be *kosher for none,* with the Jewish Christians deferring to the gentile Christians?

Peter, Barnabas, and Paul had first accepted kosher for none, but when James of Jerusalem, the brother of Jesus, demanded kosher for all, the other apostles agreed—all except Paul. He even said that the shift from kosher for none to kosher for all by Peter and the other Jewish Christian leaders was sheer hypocrisy: "The other Jews joined him [Peter] in this hypocrisy, so that even Barnabas was led astray by their hypocrisy" (Gal. 2:13). That was a crucial apostolic disagreement for Paul. You can sense his shock in that *"even* Barnabas."

Paul's outraged refusal and truculent language at Antioch may well have stemmed from residual shock at the fact that there had even been discussion about gentile male circumcision at Jerusalem. The topic was raised by those he calls, rather nastily, "false believers secretly brought in, who slipped in to spy on the freedom we have in Christ Jesus, so that they might enslave us" (2:4). Had Jerusalem decided in favor of circumcision for gentile Christians, Paul's mandate from God would have been negated. You can still sense his shock throughout all of 2:1–14.

Apart from his specific no-concession mood, what he said to Peter at Antioch was not actually in line with his own basic theology. We leave that for now, but return to this problem of the eucharistic meal in mixed Christian communities—not at Antioch, but in Rome—in Chapter 6 and find there a very different solution from a not so angry Paul. But, in any case, the result at Antioch was a serious breach between Paul, the other apostles, and "even Barnabas" that inevitably and necessarily left Paul free to go westward to the Aegean Sea on his own independent mission based primarily at Corinth and Ephesus. He went not only independently from Barnabas, but differently from Barnabas. And the difference was not just in geography, but in strategy.

PAUL'S URBAN MISSIONARY
STRATEGY

Paul was a city person, and the whole of his activity as an apostle was in cities. In this respect he was very different from Jesus, who grew up in a small village and whose public activity was rural, concentrated in villages and small towns in the countryside. Though Paul moved through rural areas as he traveled from city to city, there is no indication in Acts or his letters that he ever sought to make converts in the villages and towns through which he passed.

Paul not only focused on cities but mostly on cities that were capitals of Roman provinces: from birth in Tarsus of Cilicia, through experience in Antioch of Syria, and on to Thessalonica of Macedonia, Corinth of Achaia, and Ephesus of Asia Minor. What, then, was life like in those cities, even—or especially—in those large provincial capital cities?

Paul's cities. Travelers today in search of the past in the Mediterranean world see ruins that are "monumental"—structures that have survived for two thousand years: streets, sewers, and arches; temples, forums, and porticoes; aqueducts, fountains, and baths; odeons, theaters, amphitheaters, and hippodromes. In some cities, villas—homes of the wealthy and powerful—have also survived. We see the grandeur of the past, and it is impressive.

But we do not see how "ordinary" people lived. Their buildings and neighborhoods are gone, too poorly constructed to endure centuries of time. Few visual cues of their existence help today's travelers to imagine their lives. Indeed, it is easy to forget they were ever there. Yet it was among ordinary urban people that Paul lived and carried out his apostleship.

The "ordinary" people of that world were the vast majority of the urban population. They were the urban working class. Our list is not meant to be comprehensive, but to spark the imagination: drivers, drovers, porters, cleaners, custodians of public buildings, bathhouse attendants; construction workers, bricklayers, masons, carpenters; tanners, butchers, bakers, spinners, weavers; artisans in workshops working in cloth, leather, pottery, gold, silver, wood, and stone (remember that everything had to be made by hand); small entrepreneurs and shopkeepers selling various goods; day laborers looking for work, and sometimes not finding any.

The urban working class also included those who could not work, or could work only sporadically, for a variety of reasons: age, illness, lack of skills, shortage of employment, physical disability, and so forth. They were the destitute. Some of necessity became beggars; others were wholly dependent on the meager resources of their struggling families.

There were also significant differences within the urban working class. Some could read and write, especially if their work required it. Some would have been not only literate, but familiar with the literature of antiquity, including the Jewish scriptures among gentile God-worshipers—a group to be explained and discussed below. But most would have been nonliterate, not because of lack of intelligence, but because of lack of opportunity or necessity.

Some were more economically secure than others, perhaps because they had become successful shopkeepers or skilled artisans. Others had long-term employment by wealthy patrons, and their futures were secure so long as their patrons did not suffer misfortune or fall out of favor. But the economic differences within the working class were small compared to the gap between it and the powerful and wealthy elites.

And so we turn to imagining what the lives of the urban working class were like. To begin with, cities in the ancient world were very different from modern cities. When we think of cities today, we generally think of a "downtown," a central business and entertainment district, surrounded by residential neighborhoods and expanding as necessary into suburbs. For us, cities sprawl.

But not so in the ancient world. Cities were small in area, and for an obvious reason: they were almost always enclosed in walls. Because it was very expensive to build new walls, the population as it grew remained concentrated within the walls. Thus population density was very high, especially in the areas where the working class lived.

We illustrate with a recent "case study" of ancient Antioch, capital of the Roman province of Syria, based, with gratitude, on Rodney Stark's book *The Rise of Christianity*.[4] The population of Antioch in the first century was about 150,000, and the area within its walls was 2 square miles, which amounts to 75,000 people per square mile, or 117 per acre. To compare this to modern American cities: Chicago has 21 per acre, San Francisco 23, and Manhattan 100. But keep in mind that many people in Manhattan live "vertically"—in buildings with many stories, towering above anything possible in the ancient world.

In Antioch, as in other cities in the Roman Empire, much of the area inside the walls was used for public buildings—about 40 percent. Villas of the wealthy took up a few more percent. Thus most of the population—the urban working class—lived in less than 60 percent of the area. For them, the population density per acre was around 200—twice that of Manhattan, but without Manhattan's tall high-rises.

Though the buildings in which the working class lived have not survived, we know from literary sources and archaeological traces that most lived in multistoried tenements. At most, they were five or six stories high, the practical limit of ancient residential construction. Most people were tenants rather than owners; we do not know if there were ancient "condo" arrangements.

Many families lived in one room, all that they could afford, and mostly used it for sleeping and storage. For them, daylight hours were spent working and outdoors, except when weather or illness made it impossible.

In these densely populated tenement areas, lack of sanitation was an enormous problem. Those of us who have traveled in that part of the world have often marveled at the sophisticated plumbing in the villas of the wealthy: running water, indoor toilets, hot water for baths, and so forth. Not so in tenement areas. Tenements did not have running water. Water for household use had to be carried, most often up many floors. Toilet facilities were pit latrines and chamber pots, usually emptied into gutters in the narrow streets.

The lack of sanitation bred not only stench, but insects and diseases. Mortality rates from disease were high everywhere in the ancient world, but even higher in cities—so high that cities could not have survived without a steady influx of people from the countryside. Of this, there was plenty. The major reason was an economic policy of the Roman Empire: agriculture was being systematically commercialized. Once, families had worked a small piece of their own land to provide for their needs, but that was changing as land increasingly passed into the hands of large landowners who employed workers to produce crops for commercial sale.

The result was a virtually forced migration to cities. Thousands from rural areas who had become landless, whose labor was no longer needed, or who were unable to produce enough income for their families to live on moved to cities. A majority of the urban working class were thus newcomers and strangers to each other. Moving to a city meant the loss of traditional communities of support provided by extended families and lifelong residency in a village. Moreover, because of the high death rates within cities, many who moved there with families soon found themselves without family.

Migration to cities also involved people of many different linguistic and ethnic groups. Antioch, with its population of 150,000 on 2 square miles, included eighteen ethnic quarters. Misunderstanding, rivalry, and enmity were endemic and often resulted in riots. Thus, as Stark concludes, the cities of Paul were places of "misery, danger, fear, despair and hatred,"[5] despite the glory suggested by the last remains of their monumental structures.

This is the setting in which Paul conducted his urban mission. He was able to do so in part because he practiced an urban trade: he was a tentmaker. We should not think of tents in the modern sense of what campers use or even in the premodern sense of what nomads lived in. Nomads did not come to cities to buy tents. Rather, a tentmaker was an awning maker, using cloth or skins or both. Tents as awnings were in considerable demand in Paul's world of the Mediterranean sun, and his skill gave him mobility. His tools were light and could be carried with him, and he could find employment in virtually any city. We find him working, for example, in the shop of Aquila and Priscilla at Corinth: "Because he was of the same trade, he stayed with them, and they worked together—by trade they were tentmakers" (Acts 18:3).

Paul's audiences. What did Paul do in those predominantly capital cities? Who were his primary or focal audience? We must, once again, read Luke's account in Acts very carefully to distinguish information from interpretation. Luke superimposed the missionary strategy of Barnabas on Paul, but Paul, having learned it under Barnabas, set out to change it quite drastically when he went out on his own.

Luke's account of Paul's missionary strategy sends him immediately to the Jewish synagogue in city after city in order to convert his fellow Jews to Christian Judaism: Pisidian Antioch (13:14),

Iconium (14:1), Thessalonica (17:1), Beroea (17:10), Athens (17:17), Corinth (18:4), and Ephesus (18:19; 19:8). Luke's understanding of Paul's missionary strategy is clear and consistent—in every city he always starts in the synagogue with his fellow Jews. But is that what Paul actually did? Is that what actually happened?

Paul's own account of his mission always insists that he was divinely called for and to the "Gentiles." First, at the very start, in Damascus, he says God chose "to reveal his Son to me, so that I might proclaim him among the Gentiles." Second, that is how he always describes his vocation thereafter, for example, in Romans: "among all the Gentiles" (1:5), "among the rest of the Gentiles" (1:13), "to win obedience from the Gentiles (15:18). Finally, his specific titles for himself in that same letter are: "an apostle to the Gentiles" (11:13) and "a minister of Christ Jesus to the Gentiles" (15:16). If, therefore, Paul went, as in Luke's Acts, to convert Jews in the synagogue, he was disobeying his missionary mandate from God and contradicting his own understanding of his destiny.

Furthermore, he would also have been contravening the decision agreed on between himself and all the other apostles at Jerusalem around the year 50 CE. As you will recall from above, the question there was whether gentile males who converted to Christianity had to undergo circumcision. The general apostolic agreement was that circumcision was not required of them. But that same apostolic council also created two separate missions, one to Jews and one to Gentiles, and in Galatians Paul repeats that three times, with emphasis on his own role for the Gentiles:

1. I had been entrusted with the gospel for the *uncircumcised* [*Gentiles*], just as Peter had been entrusted with the gospel for the circumcised [Jews]

2. (for he who worked through Peter making him an apostle to the circumcised also worked through me in sending me to the *Gentiles*),

3. and . . . James [the brother of Jesus] and Cephas [Peter] and John [brother of James and son of Zebedee] gave . . . the right hand of fellowship, agreeing that we should go to the *Gentiles* and they to the circumcised. (2:7–9)

Our conclusion is that Paul could never have begun in each city by going to the synagogue to convert *Jews* to Christian Judaism. But he could have gone to the synagogues to do something else—something more in keeping with his divine mandate at Damascus and his human mandate at Jerusalem. Put another way, who are those Gentiles to whom Paul went?

We usually think, from the Jewish religious viewpoint in antiquity, of two groups distinguished as "Jews" and "Gentiles" or of, as Paul says in Galatians, "Jew and Greek" (3:28). But there was actually a third option. There were also Gentiles who stayed Gentiles—if they were males, for example, they remained uncircumcised—but who became what we might call *gentile synagogue adherents*. In other words, they accepted Jewish monotheism, respected Jewish morality, family ethics, and communal values, and, most especially, attended the synagogue regularly.

We know about these groups not only from Jewish texts by the historian Josephus and the philosopher Philo, but also from ancient Jewish inscriptions. One striking if not stunning example is a list of financial donors on the synagogue door at Aphrodisias, a city east of Ephesus in modern Turkey. It has 126 names and distinguishes three separate groups: 55 percent are Jews, 2 percent are "converts," and 43 percent are those synagogue adherents who are explicitly called "God-worshipers" (9 of them were members of the city council).

But, above all, we know about those gentile synagogue adherents from Luke, and that is our present focus. Throughout Acts, Luke uses two different Greek verbs to describe these gentile synagogue adherents. The first one refers to them as the "God-fearers" or "those fearing God" in 10:2, 22, 35; 13:16, 26. The second verb refers to them as the "worshipers of God" or "the devout before God" in 13:43, 50; 16:14; 17:4, 17; 18:7. What do we learn from that Lukan data on those gentile synagogue adherents—the "God-fearers" or "God-worshipers"?

Luke repeatedly distinguishes those synagogue adherents from full Jews in the above lists: "You Israelites, and others who *fear God*" (13:16); "you descendants of Abraham's family, and others who *fear God*" (13:26); "many Jews and *devout* converts to Judaism" (13:43); "the Jews and the *devout* persons" (17:17). (Actually, of course, "adherents" were not "converts" as Luke says above in Acts 13:43.) Notice also that women are explicitly emphasized among those synagogue adherents and that some of them are important persons: "Lydia, a *worshiper* of God, was . . . a dealer in purple cloth" (16:14); "a great many of the *devout* Greeks and not a few of the leading women" (17:4).

We do not imagine that all those gentile synagogue adherents would necessarily accept full adherence to Christianity instead of partial adherence to Judaism. Some opposition is recorded: "But the Jews incited the *devout* women of high standing and the leading men of the city, and stirred up persecution against Paul and Barnabas, and drove them out of their region" (13:50). But, in any case, our proposal is that Paul went always to the synagogue in each city *not* to convert his fellow Jews, but *to convert the gentile adherents* to Christian Judaism. And that proposal explains huge swaths of Pauline data.

Paul's primary focus on "God-fearers" or "God-worshipers" explains the serious Jewish animosity toward Paul. He is doing what we might call *adherent poaching*. If he just talked to his fellow Jews, they could deride him. If he just talked to pure pagans, his fellow Jews could ignore him. But the Jewish Paul and the Jewish synagogue are struggling with one another over a third party, namely, those gentile adherents. "Stay with traditional Judaism," says the synagogue; "Convert to Christian Judaism," says Paul.

Furthermore, Paul's primary focus on "God-fearers" or "God-worshipers" explains how converted pagans could possibly understand the theology of Paul's letters—that to the Galatians, for example. They were not pure pagans, but ones already schooled in Jewish faith and thought by regular synagogue attendance and partial Jewish observance.

Finally, and maybe above all else, Paul's primary focus on "God-fearers" or "God-worshipers" explains his stunning claim after the mid-50s that "now, with no further place for me in these regions, I desire, as I have for many years, to come to you when I go to Spain" (Rom. 15:23–24). After only about twenty years—say from the mid-30s to the mid-50s—Paul is finished in the east and so turning to the west of the Roman Empire. How can he possibly make such a claim? And what does it tell us about Paul's urban missionary strategy?

He can only make that startling assertion because of his particular strategic focus, his "demographics," to use a modern term. Out of the total number of possible cities, he chose first to concentrate on unevangelized cities—"I make it my ambition to proclaim the good news, not where Christ has already been named" (Rom. 15:20). Then, within that group of "new" cities he set his sights on Roman provincial capitals. And, finally, within them he targeted gentile synagogue adherents, the

"God-fearers" or "God-worshipers" of the Acts of the Apostles. By the way, Luke himself was possibly one of them. Based on that focus Paul could, after only twenty years, claim to be finished in the eastern and ready for the western Roman Empire.

Paul's communities. Whether we think of Paul working as an artisan in a shop or scouting the local synagogue for God-worshipers (adherent poaching), both activities involved him in networks. The Gentiles attracted to Judaism to whom he spoke in synagogues would have had both gentile and Jewish friends and connections. Indeed, many of his Jewish converts may have come from this overlapping group of Gentiles and Jews. His employment in a workshop would have connected him to a primarily gentile network of the urban artisan class as well as to other Gentiles in the vicinity of the shop.

Paul's communities were small. There are two reasons for thinking so. In that above-cited study of early Christianity by Rodney Stark, his growth estimates suggest about two thousand Christians in the whole of the Roman Empire by the year 60, by which time most and probably all of Paul's genuine letters had been written. The story of Pentecost in Acts suggests a much higher figure. There we are told that on the very first day of Christian preaching "about three thousand" were baptized (Acts 2:41). But this is hyperbole. Luke, like other ancient writers often used hyperbolic numbers. The lower estimate is more realistic.

Assuming that about a thousand were in the Jewish homeland, the other thousand would have been spread out over the rest of the empire, largely in Syria, Asia Minor, Greece, presumably Egypt, and as far as Rome. Thus, in any of the cities where Paul created communities, with perhaps an exception or two, the number of Christians is unlikely to have been more than a hundred and perhaps as small as a few or several dozen.

The second reason that Paul's communities were small was space limitation. Buildings specifically designed as churches were still two to three centuries in the future, and so Paul's communities met in existing spaces. It is common to speak of "house churches," but more likely we should think of "shop churches"— that is, groups of Christians meeting in workshops, which were commonly on the ground floor of tenements and other buildings. Shops were small, most not larger than ten by twenty feet, some even smaller. Larger assemblies would be possible if one or more of the converts had enough wealth to own a villa and host gatherings there, as in Corinth. But for the most part, we should think of small gatherings. And it is possible, perhaps even likely, that there were several "shop churches" in a given city.

Paul nowhere set out to describe in a comprehensive way what life in these communities was to be like. He did not write a manual of community practice. And so there is much that we do not know. For example, though Paul does not say so, we assume they gathered frequently. Once a week? More often? The only hint we get is in a passage about the collection of money Paul was gathering from his Christian Gentiles for Christian Jews in Jerusalem:

> Concerning the collection for the saints: you should follow the directions I gave to the churches of Galatia. *On the first day of every week,* each of you is to put aside and save whatever extra you earn, so that collections need not be taken when I come. (1 Cor. 16:1–2)

We return to that collection in our Epilogue. For now, that passage implies at least a weekly gathering, but need not mean that they gathered only once a week. Indeed, given that these were small and intimate communities made up of highly committed people living in the neighborhood of a shop, we imagine that the members were in frequent contact with each other.

We know they celebrated the "Lord's Supper," for Paul mentions it in 1 Corinthians 11:20. Did they do so every time they gathered or once a week on that "first day of the week"? We know that baptism was the rite of initiation into the new community. We do not imagine that it was undertaken lightly; we imagine, but do not know, that there was a fairly long period of instruction and discernment beforehand. The portrait in Acts of converts sometimes being baptized immediately after hearing "the word" is very difficult to imagine in practice. After all, becoming part of a Christian community meant following a Lord crucified by empire and entering into a way of life that countered the normalcy of imperial civilization. In the rest of this book, we will be—directly or indirectly—reconstructing those communities from the letters of the radical Paul.

CHAPTER FOUR

"JESUS CHRIST IS LORD"

Before jesus was born—or even if he had never existed—another human being was already proclaimed Son of God and, indeed, God Incarnate within the same first common-era century and within the same Mediterranean world. In fact, almost all the sacred terms and solemn titles that we might think of as Christian creations or even Pauline inventions were already associated with Caesar Augustus, the first undisputed ruler of the Roman Empire, from 31 BCE to 14 CE.

Augustus was Divine, Son of God, God, and God from God. He was Lord, Liberator, Redeemer, and Savior of the World—not just of Italy or the Mediterranean, mind you, but of the entire inhabited earth. Words like "justice" and "peace," "epiphany" and "gospel," "grace" and "salvation" were already associated with him. Even "sin" and "atonement" were connected to him as well.

Horace asked in one of his *Odes:* "Our children, made fewer by their parents' sins . . . to whom shall Jupiter assign the task of atoning for our guilt?" His answer was Augustus, in whom Hermes-Mercury, messenger of heaven, had "assumed on earth the guise of man," and who as "our leader, Caesar," would remain with Rome unless, once more, the gods became "angered at our sins" (1.2.29–52).

Our problem is now as clear as the sunlight on a pine-clad Mediterranean hillside. All those assertions, terms, and titles were at home within Roman imperial theology and incarnated in Caesar the Augustus before they ever appeared in Pauline Christian theology and were incarnated in Jesus the Christ. So here is the question: What exactly is the fundamental difference between Caesar and Christ? Even before one commits in faith to either, how precisely does one differentiate between them? We repeat, for emphasis: What is the basic, fundamental, and constitutive difference between those divine claims and transcendental titles as made for Caesar by Rome and for Christ by Paul?

We begin this chapter by comparing descriptions from the mid-50s CE of two divine human beings. One is Jesus the Christ, the other is Nero the Emperor, and both of them proclaim that they bring *peace* to this troubled earth. That introduces how we focus our constitutive question about those common titles for Christ and Caesar in this chapter—we focus it around peace on earth.

Granted all those common terms and titles, what is the difference in *specific content* between world peace for a Roman emperor like Nero and world peace for a Jewish peasant like Jesus? In answer, we look closely at what peace meant first in Roman imperial theology and then in Pauline Christian theology. Then, we probe a little deeper by picking up those questions left as unfinished business at the end of Chapter 2.

Why does Paul insist that the justice of Christian life demands equal status for its members, especially against the standard contemporary hierarchies of class (slave/free), gender (female/male), and ethnicity (Jew/Greek)? How did Paul even imagine that claim against the traditional presuppositions of Mediterranean patriarchy and Roman normalcy?

Where did Paul's vision of the justice of equality come from? Are we imprudently retrojecting contemporary ideas of democracy, civil rights, and human rights back onto a first-century mind that was never thinking in those terms?

Beneath all those divine titles and transcendental claims just cited as common to Caesar and Christ, how does the structural core of Roman imperial theology differ from that of Pauline Christian theology—in specific content?

PEACE FOR ALL THE WORLD

In the mid-50s CE, Paul opened his letter to the Roman Christians by proclaiming

> the gospel of God . . . concerning his Son, who was descended from David according to the flesh and was declared to be Son of God with power according to the spirit of holiness by resurrection from the dead, Jesus Christ our Lord. (Rom. 1:1–4)

He then wished them:

> Grace to you and peace from God our Father and the Lord Jesus Christ. (Rom. 1:7)

But even as Paul wrote to Christian Romans about that human and divine Jesus, another author wrote to non-Christian Romans about the human and divine Nero, the new, seventeen-year-old, fourth emperor since Augustus. In his *Eclogues,* Calpurnius Siculus rejoiced:

> Amid untroubled peace, the Golden Age springs to a second birth; at last kindly Themis [Greek goddess of Justice] . . . returns to earth; blissful ages attend the youthful prince. . . . While he, a very God (Latin *ipse deus*), shall

rule the nations, the unholy War-Goddess shall yield and
have her vanquished hands bound behind her back. . . .
Peace in her fullness shall come; knowing not the drawn
sword. . . . Assuredly a very God (*ipse deus*) shall take in
his strong arms the burden of the massive Roman state.
(1.42–47, 63, 84–85)

How was it even possible—let alone credible—that the exact same terms and titles were taken by Christians from Caesar
the Augustus on the Palatine Hill in Rome and given to Jesus the
Christ on the Nazareth ridge in Galilee—or, even worse, to
the "King of the Jews" on a Roman cross in Jerusalem?

What did Paul and his communities mean when they denied
those terms and titles to Caesar and transferred them to Christ?
Was it low lampoon or high treason? If it was all a joke, why
were the Roman imperial authorities not laughing? And, if it was
not a joke, what was the fundamental difference between the
incarnate program of a Caesar and that of a Christ?

Think, for example, of those proclamations of imperial justice
and peace that accompanied the accession of Nero as *ipse deus*—
"a very God" or, better, "the God Himself"—after his accession
in October of 54 CE. What is the essential difference between
Roman peace and Christian peace? With the same transcendent
status claimed for both, what was the difference in *content* between them?

As mentioned in Chapter 2, each of Paul's seven authentic letters begins with exactly the same official and formulaic greeting.
The only slight exception is his earliest letter, and even there all
the key elements of the formula are already present. Furthermore, in all of Paul's letters except Philemon the final farewell
always mentions "peace." Here they all are:

To the church of the Thessalonians in God the Father
and the Lord Jesus Christ: Grace to you and peace. . . .

May the God of peace himself sanctify you entirely.
(1 Thess. 1:1; 5:23)

Grace to you and peace from God our Father and the
Lord Jesus Christ. . . . Peace be upon them, and mercy,
and upon the Israel of God. (Gal. 1:3; 6:16)

Grace to you and peace from God our Father and the
Lord Jesus Christ. . . . The God of peace will be with
you. (Phil. 1:2; 4:9)

Grace to you and peace from God our Father and the
Lord Jesus Christ. (Philem. 3)

Grace to you and peace from God our Father and the
Lord Jesus Christ. . . . Send him on his way in peace, so
that he may come to me. (1 Cor. 1:3; 16:11)

Grace to you and peace from God our Father and the
Lord Jesus Christ. . . . Live in peace; and the God of love
and peace will be with you. (2 Cor. 1:2; 13:11)

Grace to you and peace from God our Father and the
Lord Jesus Christ. . . . The God of peace will shortly
crush Satan under your feet. The grace of our Lord Jesus
Christ be with you. (Rom. 1:7; 16:20)

Are we able, then, to distinguish the peace-of-God-in-Christ
from the peace-of-Rome-in-Caesar by simply invoking that phrase
"grace and peace," as if the Christian but not the Roman peace
were a *charis* (in Greek), a free gift from heaven? That might work
in a Christian monologue, but not in a Christian-Roman dialogue
conducted posthumously—imagine it—between Paul and Virgil.

If Homer's *Iliad* was the Old Testament of Roman imperial
theology, Virgil's *Aeneid* was its New Testament, published under
Augustan directions after the poet's death in 19 BCE. Rome's

destiny began in heaven when the supreme god Jupiter told his goddess daughter Venus, "For these I set no bounds in space or time, but have given empire (*imperium*) without end . . . [to] the Romans, lords of the world and the nation of the toga. Thus it is decreed (*sic placitum*)" (1.278–83).

That divine "decree" or "pleasure" is simply another way of expressing divine "grace." In Galatians, for example, Paul said that God "called me through his grace" and "was pleased to reveal his Son to me" (1:15–16). Any competent Roman imperial theologian would have countered that the Pax Romana was a free and gracious gift from Jupiter, although possibly merited and maintained by continued religious piety. The goddess Victory was winged, for example, so she could go where she was graciously sent from on high.

We will have to dig deeper to answer our question about the *content* difference beneath all those same Roman and Pauline terms and titles, between, for example, the peace of Caesar and the peace of Christ. We cannot claim that it is a religious rather than a political peace, an internal rather than an external peace, a heavenly rather than an earthly peace, or even a future rather than a present peace. We already saw in Chapter 2, for example, that the peace of Christ meant the freedom of Onesimus—religiously and politically, internally and externally, on earth and in heaven, now and in the future. It is time, therefore, to look first at Caesarian peace, and then we can more clearly see how Paul distinguished Christian peace from it.

ON THE HEIGHTS OF ANCIENT PRIENE

On the mid-Aegean coast of Turkey, Friday, September 26, 2003, is predictably warm and cloudless, and we, along with the Borg-Crossan pilgrimage group, are there for two major reasons, each inseparable from the other.

One reason is that we are Americans, and it is now over a century and a half since the elder Oliver Wendell Holmes announced, "We are the Romans of the modern world—the great assimilating people. Conflicts and conquests are of course necessary accidents with us, as with our prototypes." That is a claim repeated often today—by liberals sadly and conservatives gladly—as our leaders work on those "necessary accidents" in places like Iraq. Since 2000, therefore, we go on a regular annual pilgrimage to wander and ponder the shattered ruins of "our prototypes" in the Roman Empire of two thousand years ago.

The other reason is that we are Christians traveling—but much more comfortably than he did—in the footsteps of Paul. We go to cities Paul visited, such as Antioch in Pisidia or Perga in Pamphylia. But we also go to ones Paul never visited, such as Aphrodisias in Caria or Priene in Ionia. There too we can see monuments to that Roman imperial theology against which he brought Pauline Christian theology as God's alternative vision for global peace.

That beautiful early fall morning, we come south from Ephesus to the city of Priene, which climbs up the base of Mount Mycale in a triumph of terrace over terrain. It was and is high above the Meander Plain and so—unlike Tarsus—far above marshes, mosquitoes, and malaria. The city has long been in ruins, but its mighty acropolis still towers above the ever expanding plain. And down there workers—now migratory ones from eastern Turkey—still toil in the cotton fields beneath the Mediterranean sun with little of the breeze that refreshes the heights above them.

We climb up toward the ancient city's main temple, dedicated to Athena, virgin goddess of war and wisdom—not oxymoron, but redundancy for the Greek empire and every empire before and after it. The temple complex was slowly but steadily constructed for three hundred years from the time of Alexander to that of Augustus, a tribute to the warrior goddess from one world conqueror after another. In the temple's inner sanctum Athena's cult statue was once helmeted; she held arms in her left hand and a statuette of Victory (*Niké*) in her right.

On this late September morning, Athena's great temple is indicated by only five of its original thirty outside columns. They were erected a half century ago by a local construction company to about 4 feet short of their original height. All around them is a vast array of shattered marble chunks and toppled marble drums destroyed by the area's frequent earthquakes.

We sit with our group, as we do each year, outside the temple's east end on the broken remains of the altar to meditate on a fallen beam that was once located high above the main entrance to the temple's inner shrine. It is now reconstructed on the ground at our feet, and its large Greek lettering is clearly legible across two huge chunks—two more were added by the time we returned in September 2004.

Our focus is on the inscription carved on that lintel beam when the temple complex was finally dedicated to Athena and to Augustus as well—a Greco-Roman divine marriage made, as it were, in heaven. We give it first in standard English translation, but will then discuss certain words that can be quite misleading for us:

> THE PEOPLE TO ATHENA PATRON OF THE CITY
> AND TO THE EMPEROR CAESAR THE SON OF GOD
> THE GOD AUGUSTUS

We sit there each year to think about that inscription and to focus especially on the three major titles given to the first ruler of the Roman Empire.

Imperator Caesar. Of the three titles on that inscription, the first one is *Autokrator* in Greek, that is, *Imperator* in Latin and "Emperor" in English. "Emperor" is an accurate but inadequate translation. Our group already saw the problem a week earlier in Ankara, where Augustus's own political résumé—*The Achievements of the Divine Augustus* (*Res Gestae Divi Augusti*)—was carved in Latin and Greek on the walls of the first-century Temple to Rome and Augustus. At its start, among his various military triumphs, he noted, "Twenty-one times I was named Emperor (*Imperator*)." Obviously, "Emperor" does not work there as the English for *Imperator*.

For Rome, *Imperium* ("empire") meant the legal right to take Roman forces into battle, and *Imperator* was the official titular acclamation from the legions to a victorious commander. That battle-site proclamation by his troops was the necessary prelude to the general's possible triumphal procession within the city of Rome.

But for Augustus all victorious acclamations *under* him belonged *to* him (twenty-one in all). They all coalesced, so that *Imperator* became his own first name. Inscription after inscription begins—as here at Priene—with *Imperator Caesar*. With Augustus military victory was incarnated more or less exclusively in himself—no matter who might have prevailed in the actual battle. In other words, the first—and it was always first—title of Augustus was *Imperator,* and it meant military victor as world conqueror. It meant the All-Conquering One.

Son of God. The second title on that dedicatory inscription is *Theou Huios* in Greek, that is, *Divi Filius* in Latin and "Son of God" in English. Here again we must be very careful, because failure to understand how Rome's imperial theology was incarnated in Caesar the Imperator will result inevitably in failure to understand how Paul's Christian theology was incarnated in Jesus the Christ.

Greco-Roman theology recognized immortal gods—a *deus* like Zeus or Jupiter—but also human beings who were raised to divine status—a *divus* like Hercules or Julius Caesar. Such an apotheosis or divinization was merited by the extraordinary gifts or transcendental benefits those divine humans had contributed to the world. Within that religious vision, for example, Apollo was *dei filius,* a son of the god Zeus-Jupiter, but Augustus was *divi filius,* the (adopted) son of his grand-uncle, the deified Julius Caesar. But Greek made no such distinction—both those distinct Latin categories, *dei filius* ("Son of God") and *divi filius* ("Son of the Divine One"), came out as *theou huios* ("Son of God").

It would have been impossible—yes, we mean impossible—for Paul to call Jesus *theou huios* ("Son of God") in Greek without creating a confrontational echo with that title of Rome's inaugural emperor. As we saw above, he began his letter to the Romans—yes, precisely to the Romans—by declaring the "gospel of God (*theos*) . . . concerning his Son (*huios*), who was descended from David according to the flesh and was declared to be Son of God (*huios theou*) with power according to the spirit of holiness by resurrection from the dead, Jesus Christ our Lord" (1:1–4). In that letter's opening sentences he framed Jesus's humanity as son of David with a double claim of his divinity as Son of God.

God Incarnate. The inscription's third title is *Theos Sebastos* in Greek, *Divus Augustus* in Latin, and "the God Augustus" in English. Again we see Latin's distinction of *Divus* and *Deus,* but Greek's combination of both terms in *Theos.* As we stare at that inscription, we recall that same combination on our earlier visit to the Temple of Rome and Augustus at Ankara.

There the enlarged Latin heading of Augustus's political testament reads like this: "The Achievements of the Divine Augustus, by which he subjected the world to the empire [*imperio*] of the Roman people, and of the expenses which he bore for the state and people of Rome." But around the corner on the temple's south wall, the equally enlarged letters of the Greek heading had this summary translation: "The acts and donations of the God

Augustus (*Sebastos Theos*) as left by him inscribed on two bronze columns at Rome." Nothing there about world conquest, but instead of the Latin *Divi F[ilius]*, or "Son of God," we get the Greek *Sebastos Theos*, or "God Augustus."

Stay with us for a moment as we sit amid the ruins of Priene. Think with us about that Greek title *Sebastos* rather than its Latin equivalent *Augustus*. Think about the Greek because (Caesar) Augustus—like (Jesus) Christ—has become an ordinary second name rather than a transcendental titular claim. *Sebastos* is the adjectival form of the verb *sebomai,* which means "to worship." Our pilgrimage group had met it two days earlier on an inscription about Jewish "God-worshipers" (*theosebis*) at Aphrodisias and you, dear readers, met it earlier, in Chapter 3, with Luke's "God-worshipers" (*sebomenoi*).

Sebastos, however, does not mean the "Worshiping One," but the "Worshipful One," and *Theos Sebastos* means the "God Who Is to Be Worshiped." Amid all the ancient gods and goddesses that crowd Olympus, Augustus is not some Johnny-come-lately god, but the one who (above all others?) is to be worshiped. All other divinized mortals, said Horace to Augustus, achieved that status only after death but, "Upon you . . . while still among us, we already bestow honors, set up altars to swear by in your name, and confess that nothing like you will arise after you or has arisen before you" (*Epistles* 2.1:12–17).

Roman imperial theology had no problem with a human being who was, on the one hand, Son of God and, on the other, God Incarnate. It also never imagined convening a council—at Nicea maybe?—to decide how a person could be at the same time fully human and fully divine. Roman theologians—poets and artists all—would have scorned any submission of Roman theology to Greek philosophy. And so did Paul for Christian theology in 1 Corinthians 1–4.

We already have our first and most fundamental insight into Roman imperial theology from that single inscription. It is, of course, centered on and incarnated in the divine ruler. But titles such as Son of God or God Incarnate depend on that first title of Imperator, so that it must always come first. If Paul looked up, for example, as he passed through the southeastern gate of the public forum of Ephesus, the first word he would have seen on its dedicatory inscription was the abbreviation IMP, "to the Imperator as the All-Conquering One."

That Priene inscription says nothing about peace. It simply presumed and emphasized that Caesar's transcendental titles—Son of God and God Incarnate—derived from and depended upon that first—and it was always first—title of Imperator as World Conqueror. What sort of peace derived from and was incarnated in such a divine conqueror?

FROM TENT SITE TO TEMPLE WALL

In the middle of the first century BCE, almost a century of bitter social unrest and venomous class warfare had degenerated into Rome's worst nightmare, a terrible civil war with legionary forces on both sides. It looked like it was all over. Rome was doomed, the Roman Empire was finished, and, in the horrors of its dissolution, it would destroy the Mediterranean world.

In his contemporary *Epodes* Horace asked, "Does some blind frenzy drive us on, or some stronger power, or guilt?" (7.13–14). Does Rome's inaugural and fratricidal murder of Remus by Romulus mean that "a bitter fate pursues the Romans, and the crime of a brother's murder . . . be a curse upon posterity"? (7.17–20). Now, he said, "a second generation is being ground to pieces by civil war, and Rome through her own strength is tottering" (16.1–2). Maybe Rome, "this selfsame city we ourselves shall ruin, we, an impious generation, of stock accurst," until wild animals and wilder barbarians will wander through "the ashes of our city" (16.9–12).

But, then, on September 2, 31 BCE, off Cape Actium on the northwest coast of Greece, the fleet of Octavian, the soon to be Augustus, defeated the combined fleets of Mark Anthony and Cleopatra in the last great naval battle of antiquity. Even as he pursued them to a double suicide in Alexandria, Octavian left instructions that his command tent on the northern promontory of Actium be turned into sacred ground. His own tent site itself was to become a shrine in which would be imbedded a tithe of the bronze attack rams from captured ships of the enemy.

Above that frontal display, Octavian had a declaration carved in very large uppercase Latin letters. It did not simply dedicate the shrine; it said that he had done so. Much of it is still preserved there, by the way, and, although parts recorded before World War II are now gone, others have since been discovered. In any case, we have enough to make the reconstruction quite secure:

> Imperator Caesar, Son of God [DIVI F], following the victory in the war which he waged on behalf of the republic in this region, when he was consul for the fifth time and imperator for the seventh time, after peace had been secured on land and sea, consecrated to Mars and Neptune the camp from which he set forth to attack the enemy now ornamented with naval spoils.

That inaugural proclamation gives in succinct summary the basic structure of Roman imperial theology as centered and incarnated in the emperor himself:

Religion → War → Victory → Peace

You must first worship and sacrifice to the gods; with them on your side, you can go to war; from that, of course, comes victory; then, and only then, do you obtain peace. That is the full structural sequence of Rome's imperial program, and you can find it in texts and inscriptions, coins and images, statues and temples across the entire Roman Empire.

At its core, Roman imperial theology proclaims *peace through victory* or, in this inscription, "victory" and "peace secured on land and sea," with almost a drumbeat rhythm to the Latin *pace parta terra marique* of that last phrase. Peace by victory, said Rome, and, indeed, has there ever been any alternative imperial program before or after it?

We turn next from that tent site at Actium to a temple wall at Ankara, from that very first proclamation of the *Imperator* Octavian around 31 BCE to the final one of the *Imperator* Augustus around 14 CE. We are referring once again to that text of his *Achievements of the Divine Augustus*. What is striking is how, throughout the forty-five years of his imperial rule, that structural core holds firm.

In the bilingual inscription of the *Achievements,* the same four structural elements of Roman / Augustan imperial theology reappear:

First comes *religion*. Augustus enumerates all the temples he fully restored or newly built, how he always deposited his victor's laurels in Jupiter's Capitoline temple, and how the Senate had decreed a total of 890 days of thanksgiving during his life.

Next comes *war*. "Wars both civil and foreign, I undertook throughout the world, on sea and land, and when victorious I spared all citizens who sued for pardon." For example: "The provinces of the Gauls, the Spains, and Germany from Gades [Cadiz] to the mouth of the Elbe, I pacified."

Then comes *victory*. Augustus writes of his "successful operations on land and sea" and of "victories on land and sea." For example: "The Alps . . . from the Adriatic as far as the Tuscan Sea, I pacified without waging on any an unjust war."

Finally comes *peace*. By ancestral tradition, the temple of Janus was formally and officially closed when there was peace throughout the Roman Empire. That happened, says Augustus, only twice before his time, but thrice during it. In fact, that same phrase seen above in the Actium inscription reappears here in the Ankara one:

ACTIUM (31 BCE): VICTORY . . . PEACE
SECURED ON LAND AND SEA

ANKARA (14 CE): PEACE SECURED BY
VICTORIES ON LAND AND SEA

From the inaugural dedication of his command-tent memorial in 31 BCE to the terminal declaration of his achievements in 14 CE, Augustus's incarnation of Roman imperial theology is profoundly consistent across half a century. Its structural sequence is: religion leading to war leading to victory leading to peace. Its enduring mantra was: peace by victories on land and sea. Its succinct summary was: peace through victory.

Furthermore, Augustus and Rome would not and could not have claimed to have invented that process. Their claim was only to have perfected it. Peace by victory, they would have said, is the way of the world, the destiny of nations, the normalcy of civilization, and the will of heaven. How else could one ever obtain global peace except through global victory. What other alternative is there?

It is precisely as "that other alternative" that Paul takes the message of Jesus out from the Jewish homeland and across the Roman Empire. It is precisely because of this radically opposing vision that all those terms and titles of Roman imperial theology's incarnation in Caesar are transferred and thereby transformed in Pauline Christian theology's incarnation in Christ.

Paul's alternative vision is, of course, the subject of this entire book. But here, as an introduction to what follows, we look at one imperial title that Paul transferred to Christ. It is, in a way, the most ordinary and everyday title, and Paul seems to usurp it almost casually—but he actually uses it quite deliberately, repetitively, and emphatically.

"OUR LORD" IS "THE LORD"

According to the Acts of the Apostles, Festus, the newly arrived Roman governor of the Jewish homeland, brought Paul before himself, King Herod Agrippa II, and his sister Bernice for judgment at Caesarea Maritima toward the end of the 50s. Festus told them:

> I found that he had done nothing deserving death; and when he appealed to his Imperial Majesty [Greek *ton Sebaston,* or "the Augustus"], I decided to send him. But I have nothing definite to write to our sovereign [Greek *tō Kyriō,* or "the Lord"] about him. Therefore I have brought him before all of you, and especially before you, King Agrippa, so that, after we have examined him, I may have something to write—for it seems to me unreasonable to send a prisoner without indicating the charges against him. (25:25–27)

The emperor at the time was Nero, but you will notice that he can be left unnamed as simply *ho Sebastos,* "the One to Be Worshiped," or *ho Kyrios,* "the Lord." But now comes a counterpoint, and from Paul himself.

Throughout his authentic letters, Paul regularly uses two expressions for Jesus: "the Lord" and "our Lord." Here are some examples. Jesus is "the Lord" in Romans 1:7 and 13:14, but in between he is "our Lord" in 5:1 and 5:11. Again: Jesus is "our Lord" in 1 Corinthians 1:2, but "the Lord" in the next verse (1:3); he is "the Lord" in 2 Corinthians 1:2, but "our Lord" in the next verse (1:3). And again, in 1 Thessalonians Jesus is "the Lord" (1:1), but "our Lord" thereafter (1:3; 5:9, 23, 28).

That moving back and forth between the two is a first and very important hint of Paul's purpose with this title. The One who is *our* Lord" is also quite simply *"the* Lord." So, then, presumably "your Lord"—whoever *you* are—is not "the Lord"? On the one hand, in that Roman world, the title "Lord" could be used as a sign of respect for any significant superior—for a master by a slave, for a teacher by a student. On the other, there is only one "the Lord" and that is the Roman emperor. And, therefore, to say that "our Lord" is "the Lord" is what the Romans called *majestas,* or high treason. And Paul's quite casual and consistent intermingling of the two titles—*our* Lord as *the* Lord—is itself an imperial insult.

Furthermore, Paul uses that same term, "Lord," for both Jesus and God. In 1 Corinthians 1:31 and 2:16, for example, Paul quotes from Old Testament texts in which "the Lord" refers to God. But then, in between those citations of God as Lord, appears this one of Jesus as Lord: "None of the rulers of this age understood this; for if they had, they would not have crucified the Lord of glory" (2:8). The lordship of Jesus merges with the lordship of God, because Christ "is the image of God" (2 Cor. 4:4).

An analogy might help in understanding Paul's use of "Lord" for Jesus—but please do not push it beyond the linguistic level. In German the ordinary word for a leader is *Führer* and, like all nouns in that language, the initial letter is uppercase. In itself, that titular term could be used of any leader, but in the early 1930s it was the official title of Adolf Hitler. He was not simply a leader, *ein Führer*—he was the Leader, *Der Führer*. In that specific context, to call Jesus "our Leader" or to say that "our Leader is the Leader" would have sent you straight to Dachau. As with the word "Leader" in the German context, so with the word "Lord" in the Roman context. Any exclusive and absolute usurpation of that title was lethally dangerous, because it was deliberately treasonous.

The problem for Rome was not calling others "Lord" or even speaking of "our Lord." That could be quite ordinary, innocent, and acceptable. But it was treasonous confrontation to claim that "our Lord" was "the Lord," and if for us today "Lord" is simply a quaintly archaic or flatly patriarchal title, the confrontational choice between the peace of Caesar and the peace of Christ does not thereby disappear.

If, therefore, the lordship of Caesar meant that vision of peace through victory inscribed on stone from Actium to Ankara, what was the content of the alternative lordship of Christ? Bluntly put, once more, how else do you obtain peace on earth except through violent victory?

THE JUSTICE OF EQUALITY IN CHRIST JESUS

Why was it only after Onesimus's conversion to Christianity that Philemon's *duty* was to liberate him by manumission? Why—for the radical Paul—cannot a Christian master like Philemon own a Christian slave like Onesimus? Why are Christian women and men, wives and husbands equal with one another? Why must Christians be equal with one another?

For the principle involved we go into the wider matrix of Pauline theology as noted in his letter to the Galatians. This absolutely crucial statement must be read fully, and to assist us in doing so, we set it out as follows:

> As many of you as were baptized *into Christ*
> have clothed yourselves *with Christ.*
> There is no longer Jew or Greek,
> there is no longer slave or free,
> there is no longer male and female;
> for all of you are one *in Christ* Jesus.
> And if you belong *to Christ* . . . (3:27–29)

That central triad must never, ever, be cited without those framing statements containing "into" and "with Christ" and "in" and "to Christ." Quoted *without those frames,* they might correctly deny the validity of slavery, but they also incorrectly deny the validity of the difference (as distinct from the hierarchy) between women and men, and the ongoing validity of Judaism as a religion separate from Christianity.

Some such declaration of equality was the heart of the radical transformation that was involved in Christian baptism. Paul repeats the call to equality, with only the first two examples, in 1 Corinthians—and again notice the framing process:

> For in the one Spirit we were all baptized into one body
> —Jews or Greeks,
> slaves or free—
> and we were all made to drink of one Spirit. (12:13)

For Paul, life "in Christ" or life "with the Spirit" means the exact same mode of transfigured Christian life committed to the justice of equality.

That baptismal formula commits the baptized person to the life principle that whether you come into the Christian community as Gentile or Jew, slave or free, female or male, *you are equal to one another within that community.* Hierarchical distinctions from outside are invalid inside. But is that simply an "as if" fiction, a demand that, when the Christian assembly meets and only within such a meeting, all will act "as if" they were equal? Is it the equivalent of: "We are all equal inside, spiritually, before God—but outside in the world, of course, everything goes back to normal"?

It is in answer to those questions that the letter to Philemon becomes absolutely vital. It was—as we saw—the perfect test case. Paul could have sent the Christian slave back to his Christian owner with admonitions for each: Onesimus is to obey and Philemon is to forgive. Or he could have requested that Onesimus remain as his own slave or even be freed into his care. But, no, as we have seen, Paul sends Onesimus back to Philemon so that Philemon can—that is, must—free him voluntarily as is his Christian duty deriving from his Christian baptismal commitment. *Christians cannot be equal and unequal to one another in Christ.* But that equality within the Christian assembly spills out into the streets and fills up all of Christian life. Christians are to be equal to one another inside and outside—in the assembly and out in society.

GOD AS HOUSEHOLDER OF THE EARTH

There is still one even deeper question. From where did that vision of baptism-based equality derive? If Paul is not working—and, of course, he is not—from modern ideas of general democratic equalities and fundamental human rights, whence came that concept of the justice of baptism-based equality?

First of all, other first-century Jews made that same claim for the justice of equality—and not just for Jews, but for all peoples. The philosopher Philo of Alexandria concluded his *Special Laws* with these aphorisms: "Equality is the mother of justice" and "Justice is the offspring of equality" (4.42.231, 238).

Also, in his study *On the Contemplative Life*, he explained that the Therapeutics, female and male ascetics who had abandoned urban life for a desert "monastery," did so because the city "engendered injustice by reason of the inequality which it produced, while the contrary disposition and pursuit produced justice by reason of its equality." For that same reason, the Therapeutics rejected slavery as "absolutely and wholly contrary to nature, for nature has created all free, but the injustice and covetousness of some who prefer inequality, that cause of all evil, having subdued some, has given to the more powerful authority over those who are weaker" (1.2; 2.17; 9.70).

When one of the Jewish *Sibylline Oracles* imagines what God's perfect world will look like on its arrival, it claims: "The earth will belong equally to all, undivided by walls or fences. . . . Lives will be in common and wealth will have no division. For there will be no poor man there, no rich, and no tyrant, no slave. Further, no one will be either great or small anymore. No kings, no leaders. All will be on a par together" (2:313–38). So we moderns should not think we invented everything.

We return to our question: How did Paul understand God's creation of a present beachhead for the justice of equality in this world within Christian communities?

Recall that "grace and peace" in all the greetings of Paul's seven authentic letters comes from "God the Father" (in the earliest one) and "God our Father" (in all the rest). We also have these terms: "Our God and Father" (1 Thess. 1:3; 3:11, 13; Gal. 1:4); "the God and Father" (2 Cor. 1:3; 11:31; Rom. 15:6); "God the Father" (Gal. 1:1; Phil. 2:11; 1 Cor. 8:6; 15:24); "the Father" (Rom. 6:4); "Abba! Father!" (Gal. 4:6; Rom. 8:15).

Think about the term "Father" for a moment. On the one hand, it seems an inappropriate male title for a God who is transcendentally beyond gender. Would not "Mother" be equally good or "Parent" much better? On the other hand, granted that patriarchal bias, why "Father" and not any of the many other exclusively male titles from that same world? Why not "Emperor"? Why not "King" or "Warrior" or "Judge"? Why, precisely, "Father"?

Paul's vision for the world is a transcendental projection of his vision of home and family. That is the only other model he has to work with. He does not work from universal human rights or democratic social privileges. He is thinking of the householder, who in a patriarchal society is usually the father, so we can with full integrity replace the gendered word "father" with the ungendered word "householder" or even "homemaker."

If, thinks Paul, you went into the household of an extended family, how would you judge the householder, that is, the one responsible for all and everything within those walls? What would make you praise or criticize the name, that is, the reputation, of the householder? What makes a good and what makes a bad householder?

Is there a just, fair, and equal distribution of rights and responsibilities, of duties and privileges? Are all the children well fed, clothed, and sheltered? Does everyone have enough? Do some members get far more than they need, while others get far less? Is it, in summary, a household well run for all concerned? If it is, then, indeed, one praises the name of the householder.

For Paul, the Householder of the earth-house, the Homemaker of the world-home, is God, and all people are God's dependents and God's children. God as Householder is the One who has responsibility and charge for the home's extended family.

Therefore, for Paul, the justice of equality is directly about God and indirectly about us. It is, first and foremost, about the honor and glory of a just God reflected in a just world. Paul is not thinking primarily about democracy, social justice, or human rights. He is thinking primarily about the honor and glory of

God revealed in how Christ lived and died and how the world should live and not die.

That, of course, is why there is so much family language in Paul. Christians have already taken their place in the family of God. Hence Philemon is Paul's "brother" and Apphia his "sister" in God's family (Philem. 1–2). It is also fascinating to watch how Paul moves back and forth between calling Christians "sons (*huioi*) of God" and "children (*tekna*) of God," sometimes in the very same unit. Since all Christians are "in Christ" and Christ is "Son of God," Paul emphasizes "sons of God" in the Greek of Galatians 3:26, but then he has "children of God" in the Greek of Philippians 2:15. Even more striking and revealing is how he interweaves "sons of God" twice in Romans 8:14, 19 with "children of God" twice in Romans 8:16, 21—and again in Romans 9:8. It is, for Paul, all about family values—but divine family values, and that is what makes him very, very radical.

Finally, against that background of God as Householder of our world-home, we return to Paul's emphasis on intra-Christian equality in Philemon, Galatians, and 1 Corinthians one more time. We might be tempted today to criticize Paul along these lines: "You are so narrow and parochial, dear Paul. You are only speaking about Christianity and not about the whole world."

We Americans have a Pledge of Allegiance assuring "liberty and justice for *all*," not just for Christians. And we open our Declaration of Independence by holding "these truths to be self-evident, that *all* men are created equal, that they are endowed by their Creator with certain unalienable rights, that among these are life, liberty, and the pursuit of happiness."

How might Paul have responded to those proclamations of universal and natural rights compared to his assertions of Christian rights and duties? Had he written a "Letter to the Americans," he might have maintained that, since he believed all should be Christians, he also believed all peoples should be equal. He might have asked how we were doing with equality for all the world or even for all Americans, noting the difficulties involved in his own attempts to persuade his small groups of Corinthians about it. He may even have come to the conclusion that, with regard to human equality, a sincere and effective parochialism might be preferable to an insincere and ineffective universalism.

Already, then, we begin to glimpse a Pauline alternative to Rome's program of peace through victory, namely, peace through justice. And here, we emphasize, if it is not already clear enough, that justice means distributive and not retributive justice (punishment). There will only be peace on earth, Paul claims, when all members of God's world-home receive a fair and equitable share of its bounty, when all members of God's family have enough. Do not confuse, he might have added, peace with lull.

There is, however, one major question left. If Rome establishes peace through military victory and therefore always presumes violence, what about God's peace through distributive justice? Could that be established by violence? Could the best way to guarantee justice be to kill the unjust, the best way to complete a just distribution of the earth's resources be to kill all those who will not cooperate fairly and equitably?

To answer that question, we look at a section in Paul that may have already occurred to you as an objection to everything said in this chapter so far. Once that section is properly understood, we will see clearly the full structural sequence of Pauline Christian theology in its confrontation with Roman imperial theology.

"BE SUBJECT TO THE GOVERNING AUTHORITIES"

How can Paul intend an opposition between Christian equality and Roman hierarchy, between Pauline Christian theology and Roman imperial theology, between Christ and Caesar, and then give the following advice or command in his letter to—precisely—the Romans? Here is the entire passage:

> Let every person be subject to the governing authorities; for there is no authority except from God, and those authorities that exist have been instituted by God. Therefore whoever resists authority resists what God has appointed, and those who resist will incur judgment. For rulers are not a terror to good conduct, but to bad. Do you wish to have no fear of the authority? Then do what is good, and you will receive its approval; for it is God's servant for your good. But if you do what is wrong, you should be afraid, for the authority does not bear the sword in vain! It is the servant of God to execute wrath on the wrongdoer. Therefore one must be subject, not only because of wrath but also because of conscience. For the same reason you also pay taxes, for the authorities are God's servants, busy with this very thing. Pay to all what is due them—taxes to whom taxes are due, revenue to whom revenue is due, respect to whom respect is due, honor to whom honor is due. (13:1–7)

Scholarship has given several responses to that question. Here are two of them, and, although we appreciate their validity, we wish to suggest a third interpretation of Paul's intention.

First, insofar as this could and would be taken as a general and unqualified principle, it is one of the most imprudent passages in all of Paul's letters. Looking back on how it has been used throughout Christian history, Paul might surely wish he had never written it.

Second, it was written to Rome in the mid-50s during the rather disturbed context after the death of Claudius and the ascendancy of the teenaged Nero. Its general, opening statements were intended to ground its specific, closing statements about taxes and revenues. It intends, in other words, to avoid martyrdom for wrong or inadequate reasons. A modern example is Dietrich Bonhoeffer's words to Eberhard Bethge when all in their cafe stood for the Nazi salute at news of the surrender of France on June 17, 1940. "Raise your arm!" said Bonhoeffer. "Are you crazy? We shall have to run risks for very different things now, but not for that salute." One dies a martyr not for salutes—or taxes and revenues—but for the deeper things of God in Christ.

Finally, however, we propose another interpretation of Paul's purpose, and it may well be the most important one. Remember, by the way, that the earliest manuscripts of Paul's letter to the Romans were written—like all other New Testament texts—without any division into our chapters or verses. Notice, then, how easily we tend to ignore immediate context—both before and after—in focusing on 13:1–7 as if it were necessarily and obviously a completely unified section of Paul's thought.

But watch what happens when we start Paul's conceptual section at 12:14 and then continue it through 13:1–7 to 13:10, when, in other words, that (in)famous section in 13:1–7 is read and interpreted within the Pauline context of 12:14–13:10.

Watch especially how closely that overall complex of 12:14–13:10 echoes the radical language of Jesus advocating love of enemies and negating violence against them in the Sermon on the Mount. That complex is, in fact, a Pauline version of Jesus's message in Matthew 5:39–48 and Luke 6:27–36.

First Parallel. Jesus says: "Pray for those who persecute you" in Matthew 5:44 and "Do good to those who hate you, bless those who curse you, pray for those who abuse you" in Luke 6:27–28. Paul says: "Bless those who persecute you; bless and do not curse them" in Romans 12:14.

Second Parallel. Jesus says: "Do not resist an evildoer" in Matthew 5:39. Paul says: "Do not repay anyone evil for evil" in

Romans 12:17. And: "Do not be overcome by evil, but overcome evil with good" in Romans 12:21.

Third Parallel. Jesus says: "Do not resist an evildoer" in Matthew 5:39, as just seen. The Greek verb for "do not resist" is composed of *anti + histēmi* and the major Greek lexicon of Liddell & Scott explains that verb as *"to stand against, esp. in battle, to withstand, oppose."* In Matthew 5:39, therefore, it means "to resist violently."

So also with Paul's theme of resistance in Romans 13:1–7. It concerns *violent* resistance and, if anything, emphasizes it even more than does Matthew 5:39. Watch his sequence of two Greek verbs across these two verses:

> Whoever resists *(anti + tasso)*
> authority resists *(anti + histēmi)*
> what God has appointed, and those who resist
>   *(anti + histēmi)*
> will incur judgment. . . . One must be subject
>   *(hupo + tasso)*
> not only because of wrath but also because of
>   conscience. *(13:2, 5)*

If *anti + histēmi* is redolent of (military) violence, *anti + tasso* is even more so. We refer once again to Liddell & Scott, which explains that latter verb as meaning "to set opposite to, range in battle against" and also "to set oneself against, meet face to face, meet in battle."

It comes from *anti,* which means "against," and *taxis,* which means "a drawing up, the order or disposition of an army . . . array, order of battle . . . a single rank or line of soldiers . . . to be drawn up a few lines deep . . . a body of soldiers, a squadron" and other such military dispositions for battle. Our English word *tactics,* by the way, comes from that same Greek root.

Final Parallel. Jesus says: "Love your enemies" in both Matthew 5:44 and Luke 6:27–28. Paul says:

> Owe no one anything, except to love one another; for the one who loves another has fulfilled the law. The commandments, "You shall not commit adultery; You shall not murder; You shall not steal; You shall not covet"; and any other commandment, are summed up in this word, "Love your neighbor as yourself." Love does no wrong to a neighbor; therefore, love is the fulfilling of the law. (13:8–10)

He manages to mention "love" five times in those three verses.

We can now see what is Paul's concern in 13:1–7 when it is replaced within its fuller context of 12:14–13:10. It is, of course, about taxes and revenues demanded by Rome but precisely about refusing them violently, about the specter of violent tax revolts among Christians. It is something that appalls him so much that—in rather a rhetorical panic—he makes some very unwise and unqualified statements with which to ward off that possibility.

Paul is most afraid, not that Christians will be killed but that they will kill, not that Rome will use violence against Christians but that Christians will use violence against Rome. And that emphasizes the ultimate difference between the peace of Rome and the peace of Christ.

ALTERNATIVE VISIONS OF PEACE ON EARTH

We began this chapter with a list of Roman imperial theology's divine titles and transcendental claims for Caesar the Augustus. We chose ones that most Christians might think of as specifically created for or at least uniquely attributed to Jesus the Christ in Pauline Christian theology. But we proposed that they had been confrontationally transferred by Paul from Caesar to Christ. And we asked what exactly the difference in specific *content* was between Rome's vision as incarnated in Caesar and Paul's vision as incarnated in Christ, especially with regard to peace on earth.

The crucial difference between the program of Caesar and the program of Christ is between peace through violent victory and peace through nonviolent justice. Both promise peace on earth, so the confrontation is in means and not ends—although, of course, different means would also change those common ends. Here, in comparison and contrast, are the structural cores of those two visions:

Religion → Nonviolence → Justice → Peace

versus

Religion → Violence → Victory → Peace

The common titles seen at the start of this chapter—Divine, Son of God, God, and God from God, Lord, Liberator, Redeemer, and Savior of the World—are incarnate programs. And those programs differ, as can be seen in the separate titles "Imperator" for Caesar and "Messiah / Christ" for Jesus. In each case, it is the incarnated content that counts.

Caesar not only proclaims but incarnates peace through violent victory, just as Christ not only proclaims but incarnates peace through nonviolent justice. There will be peace on earth, said Roman imperial theology, when all is quiet and orderly. There will be peace on earth, said Pauline Christian theology, when all is fair and just.

CHAPTER FIVE

"CHRIST CRUCIFIED"

"CHRIST CRUCIFIED" condenses the message of the radical Paul into two words, the first-century equivalent of a bumper sticker. Along with his concise crystallizations "Jesus Christ is Lord" and "in Christ" (the subject of Chapter 7), it is his gospel in radical shorthand.

Why was "Christ crucified" so crucial to Paul? What made it appropriate shorthand for his message? What significance, what meanings, did he see in the cross of Jesus? And how is Paul's understanding like or unlike the widespread Christian belief that the death of Jesus was a substitutionary sacrifice for sin—that he died in our place? Did Paul think this? Or did he see the meanings of the cross quite differently?

The cross and resurrection of Jesus go together in Paul's thought and message. Resurrection gave meaning to the cross, and the cross gave meaning to resurrection. Exploring the meanings of one necessarily involves the other. And so we will treat the meanings of the two in combination as well as Paul's understanding of the resurrection itself.

Any statement of the significance for Paul of "Christ cruci-fied" risks understatement, and so we begin with his own words. In his letter to Christians in Corinth in the first half of the 50s, he summarizes in four words the gospel he had taught while he was with them: *We proclaim Christ crucified* (1 Cor. 1:23). A few sentences later, he repeats the statement and makes it even stronger by adding "nothing" and "except": "When I came to you, brothers and sisters, . . . I decided to know *nothing* among you *except Jesus Christ, and him crucified*" (2:1–2). In equally em-phatic language, Paul underlines the centrality of the cross in his letter to the Galatians: "May I never boast of anything *except the cross of our Lord Jesus Christ*" (6:14).

"Christ crucified" wasn't simply information about how Jesus died. It had meaning. To use a theological term, for Paul the death of Jesus was *salvific*—it had "saving significance." The cross saves us. Indeed, for Paul, it is our salvation.

In Christian contexts today, the most common meaning of "salvation" is primarily about an afterlife—how one is saved in order to go heaven. But this is not what the term meant for Paul. Yes, Paul believed in an afterlife. But for Paul, salvation—being saved—was primarily about life before death. It was already hap-pening in this life, this side of death.

That the cross had salvific significance is implicit in Paul's con-cise "Christ crucified." It becomes explicit in passages in which he writes about Jesus's death as "for all," "for the ungodly," for "sinners," "for us":

> Jesus died *for all,* so that those who live might live no lon-ger for themselves, but for him who died and was raised for them. (2 Cor. 5:15)

> Christ died *for the ungodly.* (Rom. 5:6)

> While we still were *sinners* Christ died *for us.* (Rom. 5:8)

Salvific significance is also signaled by Paul's use of the word "sacrifice" to speak of Jesus's death. We—everybody, as the context of the text makes clear—

> are justified by God's grace as a gift, through the redemption that is in Christ Jesus, whom God put forward as a *sacrifice* of atonement by his blood, effective through faith. (Rom. 3:24–25)

Because of the complexity of this passage and the varied use of the terms "justified," "grace," "redemption," "sacrifice," and "faith" in the history of Christianity, we will wait to treat it more fully later. For now Paul's emphasis on the cross as having saving significance is the point: for Paul, the cross is our "redemption," a "sacrifice" that brings about "atonement."

"Christ crucified"—the death of Jesus—mattered greatly to Paul, as it does for Christians to this day. Crowning church steeples, displayed above altars, worn around necks, the cross is the most omnipresent Christian symbol. The cross is utterly important and rightfully remains so. Christianity without the cross is not Christianity.

TWO MISUNDERSTANDINGS

We think that Paul's proclamation of the cross has been misunderstood in two important ways. To proclaim "nothing except Christ crucified" has sometimes been understood to mean that only the death of Jesus matters. The second misunderstanding is even more widespread: for almost a thousand years Christians have most commonly understood the cross as a substitutionary sacrifice for sin.

Only the cross. When Paul's emphatic statements about the cross are highlighted apart from their context and his fuller understanding of their meanings, they suggest that all that mattered to Paul about Jesus was his death. Scholars and theologians have sometimes read Paul this way, some with approval and some disparagingly. Moreover, many Christians also think this way, in part because the language of liturgies often enshrines the emphasis on Jesus's death.

But we think the notion that Paul's message was primarily or exclusively about the death of Jesus and not his life is highly unlikely. Indeed, we find it impossible to imagine. As an illustration, imagine a conversation between Paul and someone he sought to convert. Imagine, for example, Paul's conversation with Lydia (Acts 16:13–15).

Paul and Lydia meet at a Jewish prayer gathering outside the city walls of Philippi in northern Greece. From the city of Thyatira in Asia Minor, she is a dealer in purple cloth (a luxury item in the Roman world) and at least somewhat wealthy. Intelligent, competent, and cosmopolitan, she is also one of the gentile God-worshipers attracted to Judaism (whose importance for Paul we emphasized in Chapter 3). In contemporary terms, Lydia is "a seeker."

Now imagine Paul telling Lydia about Jesus. Imagine, also, that he focuses on "Christ crucified" (and also, of course, on "Jesus Christ is Lord"). One cannot imagine the conversation going very far before Lydia asks, "Well, this Jesus you talk about who was crucified and then raised from the dead, what was he like?" Paul says, "Never mind what he was like—what really matters is that he was the Son of God who was crucified and died for your sins." Such an answer would have had no meaning for her. It would have been a conversation stopper.

For Paul to have told her about Jesus's death would have had no meaning unless he also told her about what Jesus was like, about the kind of person he was. What was this person like who got crucified? What did he stand for that led to his execution by the powers that ruled his world and then his resurrection by God? Who was the Jesus who is now Lord? Proclaiming "Christ crucified" could not (and still cannot) exclude talking about what Jesus was like, what he taught, and what he stood for.

The cross as substitutionary sacrifice. The second misunderstanding of Paul's emphasis on the cross is even more important. For many centuries, the death of Jesus has been understood by most Christians as a *substitutionary sacrifice* for sin, as a *substitutionary atonement,* as this theological understanding is called.

This way of seeing the death of Jesus is very familiar. Most Christians today, and most non-Christians who have heard anything about Christianity, think that the cross means, in slight variations:

Jesus died for our sins.

Jesus is the sacrifice for sin.

Jesus died in our place.

Jesus is the payment for sin.

For this understanding, the notions of punishment, substitution, and payment are central. We deserve to be punished by God for our sins, but Jesus was the substitute who paid the price. The issue is how we may be forgiven by God for our sin and guilt.

In our time, some Christians vigorously defend this understanding as the crucial center of the Christian gospel. Others are uncomfortable with it, troubled by the notion that God required a blood sacrifice and that Jesus was it. Some are not sure what to make of it, and others haven't thought much about it. But most take it for granted that this is the orthodox Christian meaning of the death of Jesus.

But this understanding is less than a thousand years old. It first appeared in 1097 in a theological treatise by Anselm of Canterbury. Its Latin title, *Cur Deus Homo?* which means "Why Did God Become Human?" states its purpose. Why did God need to become incarnate in Jesus? Anselm answers his question with the following argument:

Because of our disobedience to God, we are all sinners.

Forgiveness requires that compensation be made. For God to forgive sin without payment would imply that sin doesn't matter very much to God. The price of our disobedience must be paid.

But our debt to God as an infinite being is infinite. Therefore, no one who is finite can pay the price. Only an infinite being can pay an infinite debt.

Thus the necessity of Jesus. As the incarnation of God, he is that infinite being whose death as a substitutionary sacrifice for sin pays the price of our disobedience. Therefore we can be forgiven.

In the centuries after Anselm, this understanding of the cross became part of "common Christianity," by which we mean nothing pejorative or patronizing. We mean simply "what most Christians believe." For much of a millennium and into the present, most Christians, including the many who have never heard of Anselm or the details of his argument, have seen Jesus's death on the cross as a substitutionary sacrifice for sin.

Mel Gibson's 2004 movie *The Passion of the Christ* graphically portrays this understanding. Its focus on the last twelve hours of Jesus's life—his arrest, torture, condemnation, and death—affirms not only that what mattered most about Jesus was his death, but that Jesus had to go through all of this because of our sins. He died in our place. And the magnitude of his suffering was because of the magnitude of our sins. The movie's enthusiastic reception by many Christians, Protestant and Catholic, including the late pope, shows how widespread this notion is among Christians.

Many see it as the heart of the gospel. When a Christian asks, "Do you believe in the cross?" or "Do you believe Jesus died for your sins?" this is what is meant. Substitutionary atonement has become a lens through which many Christians see the meaning of the cross, a filter through which they hear the phrase "Christ crucified."

The problem is not with Anselm's argument—its logic is impeccable. The problem is that it is not what Paul meant when he made "Christ crucified" central to the gospel. Substitutionary sacrifice was foreign to his thought.

Indeed, seeing the cross of Jesus as a substitutionary sacrifice for sin is bad history, bad anthropology, and bad theology. It is bad history because it projects back onto Paul an understanding of the death of Jesus that did not exist in his time. Later in this chapter, we will explain why it is also bad anthropology and bad theology.

PAUL'S UNDERSTANDINGS OF THE CROSS

As we now turn to the meanings that Paul did see in the cross of Jesus, we make two preliminary points. First, as mentioned at the beginning of this chapter, the death and resurrection of Jesus go together for Paul. Each gives meaning to the other. The cross of Jesus would have had no meaning for Paul without his conviction that God had raised Jesus. Without this conviction, the cross of Jesus would have been for Paul just another execution, another life ended by imperial authority. Resurrection gave meaning to the cross. Paul's Damascus experience not only transformed Paul, but also transformed, necessarily, his way of seeing Jesus's death. It was no longer simply an execution, but a revelation.

Just as resurrection gave meaning to the cross, so also the cross gave meaning to resurrection. Imagine that Jesus had died a different kind of death. Suppose, for example, that he had died while selflessly and courageously treating victims of a plague and then been raised from the dead. Would his resurrection have the same meaning? Does it matter that the risen one is the crucified one?

For Paul, it most certainly matters. The cross gave meaning to Easter just as Easter gave meaning to the cross. Neither would have the meaning it does without the other. Together, they were revelation. Indeed, the plural, "revelations," is more appropriate, for they revealed more than one thing.

Our second preliminary remark concerns the meaning of the word "atonement." In Christian theology, the "doctrine of the atonement" concerns the meanings of Jesus's death. For many Christians today, atonement has come to be identified with a particular understanding, namely, substitutionary atonement. When people ask us what we think about the atonement, this is almost always what they are asking about.

But atonement has a much broader theological meaning. It needs to be reclaimed if we are to understand the atoning significance Paul saw in the cross. Like many other common Christian words, it needs to be redeemed. Atonement refers to a *means of reconciliation*. It presupposes a situation of separation or estrangement. How is the estrangement overcome? How does reconciliation occur? This is what atonement is about.

An old wordplay catches this broader meaning: atonement is about "at-one-ment." How does at-one-ment with God occur?

What role does the cross of Jesus play in this? How does his death bring about at-one-ment?

For Paul, as for the New Testament as a whole, the answer to this question is plural, not singular. A scholar recently wrote that Paul had dozens of ways of speaking about the atoning significance of the cross. That may be hyperbole, but not by much. We group Paul's understandings into three categories: the cross reveals the character of empire, the path of personal transformation, and the character of God.

AS REVELATION OF THE CHARACTER OF EMPIRE

In the first-century setting of Paul and his hearers, "Christ crucified" had an anti-imperial meaning. Paul's shorthand summary was not "Jesus died," not "Jesus was killed," but "Christ crucified." Jesus didn't just die, wasn't simply murdered—he was crucified. This meant that Jesus had been executed by imperial authority: crucifixion was a Roman form of execution. In Paul's world, a cross was always a Roman cross.

Rome reserved crucifixion for two categories of people: those who challenged imperial rule (violently or nonviolently) and chronically defiant slaves (not simply occasionally disobedient or difficult slaves). If you were a murderer or a robber, you would not be crucified, though you might be executed another way. The two groups who were crucified had something in common: both rejected Roman imperial domination. Crucifixion was a very public, prolonged, and painful form of execution that carried the message, "Don't you dare defy imperial authority, or this will happen to you." It was state torture and terrorism.

To proclaim "Christ crucified" was to signal at once that Jesus was an anti-imperial figure, and that Paul's gospel was an anti-imperial gospel. The empire killed Jesus. The cross was the imperial "no" to Jesus. But God had raised him. The resurrection was God's "yes" to Jesus, God's vindication of Jesus—and thus also God's "no" to the powers that had killed him.

The twofold pattern *executed by Rome* and *vindicated by God* appears twice early in the book of Acts. The authorities crucified Jesus, but God raised him up (2:23–24). A few verses later, in only slightly different language, it is repeated: this Jesus who was crucified by the authorities God has made both Lord and Messiah (2:36). Of course, these words are from Acts, not Paul, but we cite them to illustrate the obvious and immediate meaning of "Christ crucified."

Executed by Rome exposed the nature of the rulers of that world: they "crucified the Lord of glory" (1 Cor. 2:8), thereby revealing the character of the system of domination and violence that killed Jesus. *Vindicated by God*—raised by God—meant Jesus is Lord, and thus the powers that executed him were not. In language that confronted and countered Roman imperial theology: Jesus is Lord—Caesar is not.

This is the primary meaning of Paul's emphatic use of "Christ crucified" in its context in 1 Corinthians. In the brilliant, dense, and illuminating overture to the letter (1:17–2:16), Paul contrasts the "wisdom of God" and the "wisdom of the world" through a series of oppositions. Paul's repetitions of the terms "wise" and "wisdom" and their opposites, "foolish" and "foolishness," are like drumbeats dominating the section. "Powerful" and "power" (or "strong" and "strength") are also set in opposition to "weak" and "weakness."

Paul uses and also reverses these contrasts in an almost breathtaking way. His rhetoric, his manner of thinking and expressing himself, requires attention. To illustrate, we quote most of 1 Cor. 1:18–2:8 and include spaces between lines to suggest taking time to think through what is being said:

The message about the cross is *foolishness* to those who are perishing, but to us who are being saved it is the *power* of God. For it is written, "I will destroy the *wisdom of the wise.*"

Has not God made *foolish* the *wisdom of the world?*

For since, in the *wisdom of God*, the *world* did not know God through *wisdom*, God decided, through the *foolishness* of our proclamation, to save those who believe.

For Jews demand signs and Greeks [Gentiles] desire *wisdom*, but we proclaim *Christ crucified* [Paul's first use of this phrase], a stumbling block to Jews and *foolishness* to Gentiles,

but to those who are the called, both Jews and Greeks [Gentiles], Christ the *power* of God and the *wisdom of God*.

Note that Christ as the "power of God" and the "wisdom of God" is parallel to and synonymous with "Christ crucified"— and it is foolishness to the wisdom of this world.

But the foolishness and weakness of God are wiser than the wisdom and power of this world:

For *God's foolishness* is *wiser* than *human wisdom*, and *God's weakness* is stronger than *human strength*.

God chose what is *foolish* in the *world* to shame the *wise;* God chose what is *weak* in the *world* to shame the *strong*.

God chose what is *low and despised* in the world, things that are not, to reduce to nothing things that are.

God is the source of your life in Christ Jesus, who became for us *wisdom from God*.

Note that Paul again identifies "Christ Jesus" as the "wisdom from God," which he again emphatically connects with "Christ crucified," this time with the phrase "Jesus Christ, and him crucified":

> When I came to you brothers and sisters, . . . I decided to know nothing among you except *Jesus Christ, and him crucified* . . . so that your faith might not rest on *human wisdom* but on the *power* of God.

The passage concludes with one more contrast between human wisdom—the wisdom of this world—and God's wisdom:

> Among the mature we do speak *wisdom*, though it is *not a wisdom of this age or of the rulers of this age*, who are doomed to perish. But we speak *God's wisdom*, secret and hidden, which God decreed before the ages for our glory. None of the rulers of this age understood this; for if they had, they would not have crucified the Lord of glory.

In this dazzling passage, the primary contrast is between the wisdom of God and the wisdom of this world—a contrast also expressed as the foolishness of God versus the wisdom of this world. God's wisdom—"Christ crucified"—is foolishness to the world, and the world's wisdom is opposed to God's wisdom.

What did Paul mean by the wisdom of this world? Because Paul uses the word "Greeks" for "Gentiles" in the phrase "Greeks desire wisdom" (1:22), some have thought that he had Greek philosophical wisdom in mind. But that is far too narrow an understanding of the wisdom of this world, and also wrong. Greek philosophy didn't kill Jesus. Roman imperial authority did.

Paul says so himself. The wisdom of this world is not Greek philosophy, but the "wisdom of this age" and the wisdom "of the rulers of this age." The wisdom of this world, which "crucified the Lord of glory," is the wisdom of the present age and the rulers of the present age.

In Paul's historical setting, that meant Rome, of course. But it meant more than Rome. The issue was not simply *Roman* imperial authority, as if Rome were worse than most empires, and that a Jewish or Christian empire would be better. Paul did not simply indict Rome, but what he saw in it: Rome embodied the wisdom of this world—the *normalcy of this world*, the way life most commonly is, the way things are.

The *normalcy of this world* refers to the most common form of human society since the development of large-scale agriculture and the concentrations of populations it made possible, beginning in the fourth millennium BCE. What emerged is what we and others call in shorthand "domination systems," societies ruled by a few who used their power, wealth, and "wisdom" to shape the social system in their own self-interest.

The few dominated the many—and they achieved their domination thorough violence and the threat of violence. Peace—stability—came through victory and conquest, what we called in Chapter 4 Roman imperial theology. Domination systems existed (and exist) in larger and smaller forms, ranging from empires to petty kingdoms. What they shared in common was domination through power, including violence and the threat of violence. How else are kingdoms and empires created and maintained? This, along with the ideology that legitimates it, is the wisdom of this world.

Paul's indictment of the wisdom of this world is straightforward: the rulers of this age "crucified the Lord of glory." The wisdom of this world—its normalcy as domination through violence—stands in opposition to the wisdom of God. The cross reveals the wisdom of this world as foolishness—and we note that the Greek word behind "foolish/foolishness" is the root from which we get "moron" and "moronic." Compared to the wisdom/foolishness of God, the wisdom of this world is moronic, stupid. And worse, it is not only stupid, but brutal and murderous.

This is also the meaning of Paul's emphasis upon Christ crucified in Galatians. Immediately after the words quoted early in this chapter, "May I never boast of anything *except the cross* of our Lord Jesus Christ," he continues, *"by which the world has been crucified to me, and I to the world"* (6:14). The world—the world of imperial normalcy—had been crucified for Paul, had come to an end. And he had been crucified to that world; he died to that world.

Though the next text is from one of the disputed letters and thus probably not written by Paul, it is consistent with this understanding. Perhaps in the 80s, some twenty or more years after Paul was executed, the author of Colossians wrote that, in the cross, God "disarmed the rulers and authorities and made a public example of them, triumphing over them in it" (2:15). How did the cross make "a public example" of them? It revealed the character of empire, disclosing the moral bankruptcy of the domination system and the wisdom of this world that legitimated it.

Like the story of the exodus, "Christ crucified" and "Jesus is Lord" called people to center their lives in God rather than living under the pharaohs of this world. And like the exodus story, its meaning was both personal and political. It was personal in that Paul called his hearers to center their lives in God as known in Jesus rather than accepting and living by the wisdom of this world. This is the path of personal transformation. And it was political in that it subverted the normalcy of a world of domination sustained by violence. It indicted its rulers: they crucified "the Lord of glory." And further, it committed Paul and his communities to a very different vision of how things should be.

AS REVELATION OF THE WAY:
PARTICIPATORY ATONEMENT

For Paul, Christ crucified and risen revealed the way to new life "in Christ." Here it functions as a metaphor for the path of personal transformation: it involves an internal death and resurrection, dying to an old identity and way of life and rising into a new identity and way of life.

This understanding emphasizes at-one-ment through participation. We participate in the death and resurrection of Jesus, die and rise with Christ, and thereby enter a new life in Christ. Participatory atonement does not mean Jesus died for us, and therefore we don't need to. Instead, it means we are to die and rise with Christ. It is metaphorical language for a process of radical internal change.

This was Paul's own experience. He expresses it most concisely in a single sentence in his letter to the Galatians. About himself, he writes, "I have been crucified with Christ; and it is no longer I who live, but it is Christ who lives in me" (2:19–20). Paul's "crucifixion" is metaphorical; though Jesus was literally crucified, Paul had not been. Its metaphorical meaning, its more-than-literal meaning, is clear: Paul had experienced an internal crucifixion, an internal death. The old Paul had died, and a new Paul had been born: "It is no longer I who live, but it is Christ who lives in me."

Crucifixion and resurrection, dying and rising, are radical images of internal transformation. The difference is as great as the difference between life and death, and the path leads through death to life. Dying and rising with Christ is the means to life "in Christ," a phrase Paul uses over a hundred times in his letters. He uses the synonymous phrase "in the Spirit" more than fifteen times. The phrases refer to an identity and way of life centered in Christ, in the Spirit.

Paul's transformation involved an "identity transplant"—his old identity was replaced by a new identity "in Christ." We will quite often refer to this "identity transplant" as a "Spirit transplant." We have in mind an analogy to modern medicine's heart transplant, in which an old heart is replaced by a new heart. In Paul's case, his spirit—the old Paul—had been replaced by the Spirit of Christ: "It is no longer I who live, but it is Christ who lives in me."

This is central to what we meant in Chapter 1 when we spoke of Paul as a Jewish Christ mystic. He not only had ecstatic experiences of the risen Christ, but had become one with Christ by dying and rising with him. His identity was now a mystical identity "in Christ." Paul had had a Spirit transplant.

Paul uses the language of participatory at-one-ment not just about himself, but also for all who would live their lives "in Christ." In his letter to Christians in Rome, he writes about dying and rising with Christ as the meaning of baptism, the ritual of initiation into the new life "in Christ":

> All of us who have been baptized *into Christ Jesus* were baptized *into his death.* Therefore we have been buried with him by baptism *into death,* so that, just as Christ was *raised from the dead* by the glory of the Father, so we too might walk in *newness of life.* (6:3–4)

Being baptized symbolized joining Jesus in his death, being "buried with him by baptism into death." It was followed by resurrection: "just as Christ was *raised from the dead* . . . so we too might walk in *newness of life*"—the newness of life that results from a Spirit transplant through dying and rising with Christ.

Paul also writes about internal transformation through participation in the death of Jesus using the language of sacrifice:

> I appeal to you therefore, brothers and sisters, by the
> mercies of God, *to present your bodies as a living sacri-*
> *fice,* holy and acceptable to God, which is your spiritual
> worship. (Rom. 12:1)

To present one's body, one's self, as "a living sacrifice" is an image
of dying—of giving up one's life as in a sacrifice, offering one's
life as a gift to God. The result is transformation and renewal:

> Do not be conformed to this world, but be *transformed*
> by the *renewing* of your minds, so that you may discern
> what is the will of God—what is good and acceptable
> and perfect. (Rom. 12:2)

"This world," to which we are not to be conformed, is not the divinely created world of nature. That world is good. Rather, as in
1 Corinthians 1–2, "this world" is the world organized in accord
with the "wisdom of this world"—the humanly created world of
imperial normalcy with its conventions of domination, injustice,
division, and violence.

"Do not be conformed to 'this world,'" is followed immediately by "but be *transformed* by the *renewing* of your minds."
"Mind" here refers to more than our thinking function, our in-
tellect and rational faculties, though it includes them. It refers to
how we "see" the world and our lives in a more comprehensive
sense. Personal transformation includes a transformed way of
seeing "this world."

The result of this transformation and renewal is the abil-
ity to "discern the will of God." Obviously, the will of God is
very different from conformity to "this world." The personal
transformation brought about by presenting oneself "as a living sacrifice" thus also had a political meaning. To refuse to be
conformed to the wisdom of this world is to stand against it. Just

as "Jesus is Lord" is both personal and political, so is dying and rising with Christ.

To conclude, this understanding of "Christ crucified" reveals the way of becoming "in Christ." The way, the path of transformation, is dying and rising with Christ. In this sense, Paul would agree with the affirmation in John's gospel: Jesus is "the Way" (14:6). The way of at-one-ment is what we see in Jesus. And we participate in atonement by following "the Way" we see in Jesus: the path of dying and rising.

AS REVELATION
OF GOD'S CHARACTER

Paul often speaks of Jesus dying "for others" and as a "sacrifice." Our central claim is that this understanding of "Christ crucified" sees it as a revelation of the depth of God's love and Christ's love for us.

The two—God's love and Christ's love—are integrally related for Paul. He saw Jesus as the *decisive revelation of God,* a conviction that he shared with early Christianity generally. Jesus reveals what God is like. In Jesus, we see what can be seen of God in a human life. The claim has been central to Christianity ever since—indeed, it defines Christianity.

As the decisive revelation of God, Jesus reveals what has often been called the "nature" and "will" of God. We use instead the words the "character" and "passion" of God. We prefer their more dynamic resonance, even as we seek to name the same qualities. What is God's character? What is God like? And what is God's passion? What is God passionate about?

Paul's answer is that the death of Jesus—Christ crucified—reveals God's character as love and God's passion as the world. Before we turn to the positive meanings of the language of this, our central claim, we revisit an important misunderstanding announced earlier in this chapter. We do not think that Paul's language about Jesus dying "for others" and as a "sacrifice" means his death is a substitutionary sacrifice—payment for human sin.

When language such as Christ dying "for the ungodly," "for us," "for all," and as "a sacrifice of atonement" is heard within the framework of substitutionary atonement theology, it means Jesus died for our sins—he took upon himself the punishment we all deserve. He satisfied the debt we owe to God. He was punished in our place. It is this almost automatic set of associations that we invite you to set aside in order to create the possibility of hearing this language anew.

Dying "for" someone and "sacrifice" do not in themselves imply substitution. This is true in ordinary language and also in the Bible. In ordinary language, when people talk about somebody dying "for" somebody, they seldom if ever mean *in that person's place*. Rather, they mean *for that person's sake or benefit*. A parent risks her life and dies in order to save her child from a burning house. A soldier leaps on a grenade in order to save the lives of his buddies. One might say that the mother and the soldier died *instead* of the child and the buddies, but one wouldn't mean as a "substitute." Rather, they gave up their lives for the sake of others. They died that others might live.

Thinking about three twentieth-century martyrs makes the same point. Archbishop Oscar Romero—advocate of the poor and critic of the ruling class in El Salvador, killed by an assassin sent by the powerful—died because of his love for the Salvadoran people. In this sense, he died *for* them. Dietrich Bonhoeffer, executed because of his involvement in a plot to overthrow Hitler, died because of his love for the German people and those they victimized. Martin Luther King Jr. was killed because of his love for his people and his passion for a different kind of world.

In these examples, dying *for* others does not mean dying *in their place.* Rather, these martyrs died because of their love for their people and their passion for a different kind of life for their people. Love and passion led them to their deaths. Their deaths were an epiphany of the depth of their love and passion.

In ordinary language, the word "sacrifice" is often used in the same way. In the examples above, the mother sacrificed her life to rescue her child, the soldier sacrificed his life to save his friends, Romero sacrificed his life for the Salvadoran people, and so on. Once again, there is no notion that these people died as substitutes for somebody else—they sacrificed their lives, but not because a substitute was required.

We move from ordinary language to the anthropological meaning of sacrifice, namely, as a ritual practiced in many pre-modern societies, including the world of the Bible. "Sacrifice," as the Latin roots of the word suggest (from *sacrum facere,* "to make sacred"), meant *making something sacred by offering it to God.*

In the ancient world, sacrifices most often involved animals. In some cultures there were also sacrifices of grain and precious objects. What they had in common was that they were *gifts to God.* The sacrifice of animals often involved a meal as well. The animal was offered to God, made sacred by being given to God, and then portions of it were eaten by those offering the sacrifice—the meal became a sacred meal, a meal with God. Sacrifice, gift, and meal commonly went together.

Sacrifices served different purposes. Some were sacrifices of thanksgiving. Nothing was wrong, nothing was asked for, gratitude alone was the motive. There were sacrifices of petition, in which something was wanted from God. These were most often offered in times of community peril. Some were sacrifices of reconciliation, a means of repairing or overcoming a breach in the relationship with God. Here the dynamic of gift and meal is especially evident. On the level of human interaction, how do you mend a relationship that has been broken? How do you "make up" with someone you have wronged? You give a gift or share a meal, or both. So also sacrifices as a means of reconciliation were about giving a gift to God and sharing a meal with God. Together they were a means of at-one-ment: becoming one with God by eating sacred food with God.

Sacrifice was not about substitution. When an animal was sacrificed, the notion was not that God was punishing an animal instead of a person; it was not about an animal suffering and dying instead of a human being. The point is that Paul's language about Jesus's death as a dying "for us," as a "sacrifice," does not in itself mean that Jesus was being substituted for us. Indeed, we need to make the statement stronger. To see Paul's understanding of the death of Jesus as a substitutionary sacrifice for sin is to import into the notion of sacrifice a meaning that it did not have in the ancient world, including the world of Paul. Indeed, substitutionary atonement theology is completely counter to the thought of the radical Paul.

So we return to our central claim. When Paul speaks of Jesus dying for others and as a sacrifice, he uses this language to refer to the depth of God's love and Christ's love for us. Paul's claim is that God's character and passion are revealed in Jesus. What we see in Jesus reveals what God is like.

Hence Paul can speak of Christ's love for us and God's love for us interchangeably. And he often does so in passages about the meaning of the cross. The three—God's love, Christ's love, and the cross—are combined in Romans 5:6–8, one of the more important texts in Paul about Jesus dying for others, named as "the ungodly," "sinners," and "us." He says, "For while we were still weak, at the right time Christ died for the ungodly." Reflecting about how remarkable this is, Paul continues: "Indeed, rarely will anyone die for a righteous person—though perhaps for a good person someone might actually dare to die." But to die for "the ungodly" is extraordinary.

His point is that this is how much Christ loved us. Then he connects the love we see in Christ's dying for us to the love of God for us: "But God proves his love for us in that while we still were sinners Christ died for us." That "Christ died for us" reveals the depth of God's love for us, disclosing God's character as love. We see the love of God in Christ.

In different language, the same claim—that Jesus and the cross reveal God's character—is made in 2 Corinthians 5:14–21, another passage that refers to Jesus dying "for all": "He died for all, so that those who live might live no longer for themselves, but for him who died and was raised for them." The purpose of his death is that people "might live no longer for themselves, but for him" by becoming "in Christ."

The result is new life: "So if anyone is in Christ, there is a new creation: everything old has passed away; see everything has become new!" Then Paul speaks of God's role in all of this: "All this is from God, who reconciled us to himself through Christ. . . . In Christ God was reconciling the world to himself." What happened in Jesus discloses God's purpose and passion, which is reconciling the world to God. The world matters to God.

So also, in a lyrical, rhapsodic, and profound passage Paul writes about the love of God as revealed in the death of Jesus. Familiar to millions of Christians, Romans 8:31–39 begins with a question: "If God is for us, who is against us?" A series of parallel questions punctuate the passage: "Who will bring any charge against God's elect?" "Who is to condemn?" "Who will separate us from the love of Christ?"

"No one and nothing" is Paul's answer. What is the reason for Paul's confidence? The evidence that "God is for us" is the cross: God "did not withhold his own Son, but gave him up for all of us." The meaning is clear: the cross seen as the death of God's Son reveals the love of God for us. And thus the passage concludes that nothing "will be able to separate us from the love of God in Christ Jesus our Lord."

A caution: this passage uses the language of God's "agency" in the death of Jesus—God "gave him up." The language should not be literalized. When it is, it suggests that the cross was part of God's "plan"—that it was God's will that Jesus be crucified. To think this is strange and leads to a strange theology. What kind of God would require the death of this extraordinary human?

The passage is not about divine causation, as if God willed the death of Jesus. Rather, like all interpretations of Jesus's death, it reflects a post-Easter retrospective vantage point that sees a providential and revelatory purpose in it. Moreover, the power of the passage depends upon the post-Easter perception of Jesus as God's Son. The use of a parent-child metaphor emphasizes the depth of God's love: God was willing to give up "his own Son" for our benefit. *That* is how much God loves us. The death of Jesus as God's Son is a parable of God's love for us. And a parable should never be literalized—to do so would be to miss the point. Parables are about meaning.

We turn now to a passage that uses both "sacrifice" and "atonement." A summary and climax of the first three chapters of Romans, it is dense, packed with a load of freight. We (everybody, as the context of the text makes clear):

> are justified by God's grace as a gift, through the redemption that is in Christ Jesus, whom God put forward as a *sacrifice of atonement* by his blood, effective through faith. (Rom. 3:24–25)

One of the foundational texts of the Protestant Reformation, it is about justification by grace through faith, which we explore more fully in Chapter 6. Here we begin by noting that grace means "a gift," as the text itself says. God's grace, God's gift, comes through "the *redemption* that is in Christ Jesus." Like the words "sacrifice" and "atonement," the word "redemption" needs redeeming. Centuries of Christian usage associate it with sin: redemption is about being redeemed from our sins. But "redemption" in the Bible and in Paul is not about the forgiveness of sins. Rather, it is a metaphor of liberation from bondage— from life in Egypt, from a life of slavery. "The *redemption* that is in Christ Jesus" would be better translated "the *liberation* that is in Christ Jesus." We are liberated through him.

Then, like the previous passage, it speaks of God's "agency" in the death of Jesus: "*God put* [Jesus] *forward* as a sacrifice of atonement." Again, the language should not be literalized, as if God willed the death of Jesus. Rather, the language of divine agency here emphasizes the theme of God's grace: *God provided the sacrifice*. That is how much God loves us. As in the previous passage, the death of Jesus is a parable of God's grace, a revelation of God's character as love.

Finally, we come to the phrase "a sacrifice of atonement by his blood." If it does not mean substitutionary atonement, what does it mean? Did Jesus sacrifice his life? Yes. He was willing to be crucified (the words "by his blood" point to execution) because of his passion—his passion for God and for a different kind of world, the world referred to in the gospels as the kingdom of God. Did Paul think he died as a substitute? No. Did Paul think his death on a cross had atoning significance? Yes. It was about at-one-ment in the ways described in this chapter.

In short, Paul's language of Jesus dying *for others* and *as a sacrifice* reveals both the love of Christ and the love of God—the character and passion of both. Christ's love and passion led to the cross— and in that we see both his love and the love of God. So also the cross, understood as God sacrificing "his own Son" for the sake of the world, is a revelation of God's love, a parable of God's character and passion. Within this framework, the cross is a revelation of divine generosity—of God's grace and what we will call in Chapter 6 God's distributive justice, God's grace freely available to all.

We are now in a position to see why substitutionary sacrifice is not only bad history and bad anthropology, but also bad theology. What does it say about God's nature or character—about what God is like? At its heart is the notion that God is a lawgiver and judge who demands payment for sin. It emphasizes God's wrath. God's wrath needs to be appeased, placated, satisfied—choose another verb if you wish, but the need is the same. It suggests that God *required* the death of Jesus, that it was God's will, God's plan, that Jesus be killed.

Ponder what all of this suggests about the character of God, what God is like. Strict parent? Exacting judge? Demanding monarch? It turns the message of divine generosity, of grace, of God's character as love, on its head. It is difficult—we would say impossible—to reconcile substitutionary atonement with the radical Paul's ways of speaking about God as known to him in Jesus, his crucified and risen Lord.

For Paul, the cross revealed God's passion, God's will, for the world—a world different from the normalcy of "this world" of domination, injustice, and violence, all legitimated by the "wisdom of the world." It also revealed the path of internal transformation, the path of becoming "in Christ" by dying and rising with Christ. And it revealed God's character, God's nature, as divine generosity, as love for all—the ungodly, sinners, us. In all of these ways, Paul saw salvific meanings, atoning significance, in Christ crucified and risen.

RESURRECTION:
GOD HAS RAISED JESUS

We have already mentioned some of the meanings Paul saw in the resurrection of Jesus as we explored the word pairs "death and resurrection," "dying and rising," "crucified and risen." Now we focus more specifically on the second word in that pair, the resurrection itself, Paul's conviction that God had raised Jesus. What did he mean when he said this? What meaning did he see in it?

Like "sacrifice," "atonement," and "redemption," "resurrection" has a common meaning held by many Christians. For them, God raised Jesus from the dead by reanimating and transforming his corpse, leaving his tomb empty, and for a limited period of time he appeared to his followers in a way that he hasn't since. The story of Jesus ascending into heaven, said by Acts to have occurred forty days after the resurrection, brought that special time to a close.

Moreover, many believe (or think they are supposed to believe) that all of this was quite "physical"—by which we mean that the tomb really was empty, that Jesus appeared to his followers in a body that could be seen and touched, that he ate with them and even cooked breakfast for them. This, or something like this, is what most people think the resurrection of Jesus means. Some believe it, some don't, and others puzzle about it.

The scenario above is based on the gospels. More specifically, it is based on combining the quite different stories of Easter in the four gospels and reading them as literal-factual narratives. This is not the place for suggesting how these stories should be read (for this, see the final chapter of our *The Last Week*). Rather, we focus here on what Paul said.

Recall that all of Paul's genuine letters are earlier than any of the gospels and are thus the first written references to the resurrection. Our point is not that earlier is better, as if Paul should be taken more seriously than the gospels. Rather, our purpose is to see what Paul said about the resurrection of Jesus without presuming the gospel accounts.

The risen Christ as an experiential reality. Paul's conviction that God had raised Jesus was grounded in his own experience. We wrote about this in Chapter 1 as we described Paul as a Jewish Christ mystic. His Damascus experience as reported in Acts plus references in his own letters affirm that Paul had experienced the risen Jesus, that, in his own words, "I have seen the Lord" and "he appeared to me." We saw this already in Chapter 3. Thus for Paul, the resurrection of Jesus was an experience. We should almost certainly use the plural, for we are confident that Paul had several experiences of the post-Easter Jesus.

That God raised Jesus is the presupposition of all of Paul's letters, but he writes about it at length only in 1 Corinthians 15. The chapter contains some surprises. Near its beginning, Paul writes: "I handed on to you as of first importance what I in turn had received" (15.3). The language most plausibly suggests that what follows is a very early Christian tradition that Paul had "received," most likely soon after his Damascus experience. Perhaps even the pre-Damascus Paul had heard this, for he knew enough about the Jesus movement to persecute it.

Then, following brief references to Jesus dying for our sins and being buried and raised, he provides a list of those to whom the risen Christ appeared:

> He appeared to Cephas [Peter], then to the twelve. Then he appeared to more than five hundred brothers and sisters at one time, most of whom are still alive, though some have died. Then he appeared to James, then to all the apostles. Last of all, as to one untimely born, he appeared also to me. (15:5–8)

There are at least three surprises. First, Paul's Damascus experience happened at least a few years after the forty days of appearances reported in Acts. Clearly, Paul regarded experiences of the risen Christ as continuing rather than being confined to that brief period of time. Moreover, his phrase "Last of all . . . he appeared also to me" need not be understood to mean that such experiences stopped with him. Rather, it probably means that the last experience he cited in the list was his own.

The second surprise is that Paul uses language associated with visions to describe the appearances of the risen Christ. He repeatedly uses the verb "appeared" not only for the experiences of Peter and the rest, but also for his experience, suggesting that they were in this sense similar. To call them visions suggests that they were not the kinds of experiences that could have been photographed, as a literal-factual reading of the gospel stories would suggest. To call them visions is also not to demean them, as if they were "only" visions. Nobody who has had a vision would ever say it was "only a vision." Rather, Paul's experience of the risen Christ carried the conviction that he was *real* and could be *known*—but *real* need not mean a transformed corpse whom others would have seen if they had been there.

The third surprise comes later in the chapter as Paul writes about what kind of body the resurrection body is: "How are the dead raised? With what kind of body do they come?" (15:35). Here he counters a belief of at least some in Corinth that resurrection means the same thing as the immortality of the soul. He answers his own question in stages, insisting throughout that resurrection is about bodies, not about disembodied immortal souls. At the same time, he also insists that the resurrected body is not simply the predeath body brought back to life.

First, he says that there are many kinds of bodies (15:38–41). Then, in a series of contrasts, he writes about the differences between physical bodies and resurrected bodies. His central metaphor compares the physical body to a seed that is sown:

> What is sown is perishable, what is raised is imperishable.
> It is sown in dishonor, it is raised in glory. It is sown in
> weakness, it is raised in power. It is sown a physical body,
> it is raised a spiritual body. (15:42–44)

The resurrected body—including the body of Jesus—is a spiritual body: raised imperishable, raised in glory, raised in power. Clearly the resurrected body is not simply a physical body restored to life. Then Paul adds: "It is written, 'The first man, Adam, became a living being'; the last Adam [Jesus] became a life-giving spirit" (15:45). The risen Christ is a life-giving spirit.

We note that all of this is in a chapter that also includes a verse often cited by some Christians to defend a physical bodily resurrection: "If Christ has not been raised, then our proclamation has been in vain and your faith has been in vain" (15:14). But the verse has a very different meaning when set in the context of the chapter as a whole. Resurrection is not about coming back to life in a form similar to one's form before death. Rather, the difference is as great as the difference between a seed that is sown and the full-grown plant that emerges.

Paul's conviction that God had raised Jesus was grounded in his own experience of the risen Christ. It was not based upon stories such as those reported in the gospels. The pre-Damascus Paul had almost certainly heard the claim that God had raised Jesus. The claim had no persuasive power until his Damascus experience. Moreover, what he says about what a resurrected body is like does not fit well with a literal-factual reading of the gospel stories. Again, this does not mean that the gospel stories should be set aside, but it should affect how we hear those stories.

The resurrection of Jesus as an imperative. For Paul, the resurrection of Jesus not only was an experience; it also contained an imperative. The imperative is seen very clearly in the immediate meaning of his experience: "Jesus is Lord." God had vindicated Jesus and thus said "no" to the authorities responsible for his execution. The conviction that "Jesus is Lord" is not an abstract theological claim, but an affirmation with an imperative: it calls for commitment, allegiance, loyalty. If Jesus is Lord, the imperative follows immediately that we should follow him, not the would-be lords of this world.

There is a second reason for the imperative as well. As Paul writes about the resurrection of Jesus in 1 Corinthians 15, he also writes about the general bodily resurrection—not just about the resurrection of Jesus by itself, but about his resurrection in the context of the Jewish hope for the resurrection of the dead. The hope for a general resurrection is not, however, an inference drawn from the resurrection of Jesus; rather, it is the *premise* for Paul's understanding of Jesus's resurrection. Twice he emphasizes this: "If there is no resurrection of the dead, then Christ has not been raised. . . . For if the dead are not raised, then Christ has not been raised" (15:13, 16).

Understanding this requires introducing the word "eschatology." Though used with a bewildering variety of meanings by scholars and theologians, its basic meaning is quite simple. "Eschatology" comes from the Greek word *eschaton,* which means "end." It has often been understood to mean the "end of the world," as if it referred to the end of the space-time universe and thus also the evacuation of the faithful to another world, namely, heaven.

But, as we saw in Chapter 4, in Jewish thought at the time of Jesus, eschatology was not about the end of the physical world, but about the *end of this age*—the end of "this world," a world of domination, injustice, and violence. Jewish eschatology, the premise of Paul's claims about the meaning of the resurrection of Jesus, was about a transformed world. The hope for the general resurrection was a hope for what we call "God's great cleanup of the world."

In this context, Paul writes about the resurrection of Jesus "as the first fruits of those who have died" (1 Cor. 15:20). "First fruits" is a metaphor from the harvest; if the first fruits have been harvested, then the general harvest has begun. This means that Paul saw Jesus as the beginning of the general resurrection.

There are at least two ways of understanding this. The first builds on Paul's expectation that the second coming of Jesus was near and might even happen in his own life time. Paul did believe this (see, for example, 1 Thess. 4:13–18; 1 Cor. 15:51–52; Rom. 13:11–12). Within this framework, Paul believed the general resurrection was *not* happening *yet,* but would happen *soon.* In scholarship, this is called "imminent eschatology." It would all happen soon. About this, Paul was obviously wrong. Candidly, we grant that most scholars see it this way.

We understand the resurrection of Jesus "as the first fruits of those who have died" quite differently. We see it is an affirmation that the resurrection of Jesus means that the general resurrection has already begun. God's great cleanup of the world is already under way. The imperative follows that we are called to participate in it. The general resurrection is about God's passion for justice in this world—and we are to participate in God's creation of a transformed world. Participatory eschatology, or collaborative eschatology, sees eschatology as process rather than as instantaneous event.

Thus for Paul, Christ crucified and risen had both personal and political meanings. In its personal aspect, it was the path of transformation: we are transformed by dying and rising with Christ, by undergoing an internal death and receiving a Spirit transplant, so that it is no longer we who live, but Christ who lives in us. As a political statement, it proclaimed that Jesus was Lord and Caesar was not. And it proclaimed that God's great cleanup of the world had begun. Participatory atonement and participatory eschatology go together in the thought and message of the radical Paul.

CHAPTER SIX

"JUSTIFICATION BY GRACE THROUGH FAITH"

THE TITLE OF THIS CHAPTER—"justification by grace through faith"—is another important phrase from Paul, another of his concise crystallizations of the gospel. As mentioned in Chapter 1, it is especially important for Protestants, one of the battle cries of the Lutheran Reformation: we are saved *sola Scriptura, sola gratia, sola fides*—by Scripture alone, by grace alone, and by faith alone. It was also central to the Calvinist Reformation: salvation is the result of God's grace, not the product of human decision.

ROMAN PAUL, NOT REFORMATION PAUL

Paul spoke about justification by grace through faith in letters to Christians in Galatia and Rome. In this chapter, we focus on his letter to the Romans, important for more than one reason. It is his longest letter—only 1 Corinthians is a close rival. It is also the only letter he wrote to a community that he had not been to and did not know in person. Thus it is also the only letter in which he presents a comprehensive treatment of his understanding of the significance of Jesus and the gospel. The purpose of the letter was to introduce himself and his way of seeing things to a community that he planned to visit. Justification by grace through faith is the climax of the first section of the letter.

Before we turn to what the radical Paul meant with the phrase, we begin by noting a common Christian understanding, especially among Protestants. First, the issue concerns primarily the *next* life—how do we get to heaven? What will be the basis for God's judgment? Will we be judged on the basis of "works" and "the law," that is, on the basis of our deeds? Or on the basis of "grace" and "faith," commonly understood as "what we believe"? What matters more to God, behaviors or beliefs? For many Christians since the Reformation, the answer has been *faith as beliefs*, with, of course, an effort at good behavior added in.

Second, as the previous question implies, "works" and "the law" are contrasted to "grace" and "faith," so that the issue often becomes faith versus works. Third, this understanding is often implicitly or explicitly anti-Jewish, because it identifies "works" and "the law" with Judaism, as if "the law" were primarily "the Jewish law." Moreover, in Protestant polemics against Roman Catholics over the centuries, Catholicism has often been seen as a religion of "works" compared to Protestantism as a religion of grace and faith.

All of this is a serious misunderstanding of what Paul meant. When he spoke of justification by grace through faith, he was not thinking about how we get to heaven, but about transformation of ourselves and of the world in this life here below. Moreover, when he contrasted faith and works, he was not thinking of *faith-without-works*—which cannot exist because faith always includes works—but about *works-without-faith*, which, unfortunately, exists all too often—sometimes from habit or guilt, sometimes from thoughtless repetition or calculated hypocrisy.

In this book, and especially in this chapter, we will speak often of ways in which Paul has been and still continues to be misunderstood. How can we think we understand him so much better than others past and present? Here is our basic principle of interpretation: *get Paul and his letter to the Romans out of the sixteenth-century polemical Reformation world and back into the first-century imperial Roman world.* It is incorrect and begets misunderstanding to read Paul for what he was not: a Lutheran Protestant criticizing Roman Catholicism or, worse still, a Christian criticizing Judaism. It is correct and avoids misunderstanding to read him for what he was: a Christian Jew within covenantal Judaism criticizing Roman imperialism. We must read his letters within their original situation and Paul's original intention. And as introduction to that process of a correct reading of Romans in this chapter, think about this question.

Small libraries could be filled with discussions and commentaries on Romans whose cumulative results have rendered it almost incomprehensible to ordinary modern readers. Yet, no matter how profound its theology may be, it had to be comprehensible to the artisan communities and shop churches in Rome to whom it was written. It was carried to them, as we saw in Chapter 2, by a deaconess named Phoebe. She would have had to carry it from one Roman community to the next, read it, explain it, and answer questions about it.

Think about that for a moment. If Romans was as abstruse as commentators have made it over the centuries, Phoebe would need to have been an even greater theologian than Augustine or Aquinas, Luther or Calvin. Or, with no disrespect to Phoebe, have we made a letter that was surely intelligible to its communities into one deeply unintelligible to us? It is possible, we should remember, to be simple and profound at the same time. Jesus always was, and so, actually, was Paul—even, or especially, in his letter to the Christian communities at Rome.

TO HEAL A DIVIDED WORLD

We saw, in Chapter 2, that intra-Christian equality disallowed the standard Roman hierarchies of free over slave or male over female. And, in Chapter 4, it was the Christian baptismal commitment cited in Galatians 3:27–29 that grounded a radical vision of equality against the standard contemporary divisions of ethnicity, class, and gender. But all of that concerned only the Christian communities themselves. What about the great big world outside of those small assemblies?

That is precisely the subject of Romans. It concerns God's passionate desire to heal a broken world, to end the normalcy of injustice founded on violence, and to bring about a unified and peaceful earth. And that divine program is immediately emphasized by the structural sequence of the letter.

Apart from the introduction in 1:1–15 and conclusion in 15:22–16:27, the letter concerns the unification of the three great divisions in Paul's world. First, how to unify Gentiles and Jews (1:16–8:39)? Second, how to unify Jews and Christians (9:1–11:36)? Third, how to unify Christian Jews and Christian Gentiles (12:1–15:21)? Paul begins with the widest focus and then successively narrows it to consider how the human world as civilization can become once more the divine world as creation. In summary:

1.   Gentiles and Jews (Rom. 1:16–8:39)

2.   Jews and Christians (Rom. 9:1–11:36)

3.   Christian Jews and Christian Gentiles (Rom. 12:1–15:21).

Even a very casual word count, by the way, shows that the first section is more than double the length of the next two. Our own discussion will follow and even extend that Pauline emphasis.

At this stage of our book, and with Chapter 4 fresh in mind, you will recognize the ironic impertinence of Paul prescribing God's vision for peace on earth to Christian communities in precisely Rome of all places. Under heavenly mandate from Jupiter, with divinity incarnated in the emperor and ethnic diversity merged into imperial unity, Rome had already established peace on earth—as far as it was concerned. But it was, of course, the peace-by-victory of Virgil's manifesto in his *Aeneid* and not the peace-by-justice of Paul's counter-manifesto in his letter to the Romans.

Had we but time enough and space, we would have liked to take you through Romans in this chapter the way we went through Philemon in Chapter 2. But, that being impossible, we hope that you will have a copy of the letter at hand and read along with us as we go. Or, as we like to say, when all else fails, read the text. We will focus on two major aspects: the overall structural sequence of the letter and those crucial and all too often misunderstood theological terms such as "righteousness" and "justification," "grace" and "faith," "law" and "sin," "sacrifice" and "death."

THE UNITY OF GENTILES AND JEWS

The first of these crucial and commonly misunderstood terms, "righteousness," occurs in Paul's thesis statement that introduces the central themes of Romans 1–8:

> For I am not ashamed of the gospel; it is the power of
> God for salvation to everyone who has faith, to the Jew
> first and also to the Greek. For in it the *righteousness* of

God is revealed through faith for faith; as it is written, "The one who is *righteous* will live by faith." (1:16–17)

The words "righteousness" and "righteous" in Paul and the Bible generally are most often synonyms for "justice" and "just." For example, in Amos 5:24, "Let justice roll down like waters, and righteousness like an ever-flowing stream," the two halves of the sentence are saying the same thing; "justice" and "righteousness" are synonyms. Thus in Romans 1:17, the phrase "the righteousness of God" can equally well be translated "the justice of God."

In "the gospel," Paul says in that verse, "the justice of God is revealed." But what does "justice" mean in this phrase? We call attention to two very different kinds of justice. The first leads to a major misunderstanding of Paul. In popular usage as well as often in the history of theology, justice has come to mean primarily *retributive justice,* that is, punishment. Thus God's justice means divine retribution: we deserve to be punished for failing to measure up to God's standards. But this is not what Paul meant. If it were, how could God's retributive justice, God's punitive justice, possibly be "gospel," "good news"?

There is another kind of justice that we call *distributive justice.* Distributive justice is not about just punishment, but about just distribution. In the economic sphere, distributive justice means the just distribution of the material basis of existence; in the Bible, it means the just distribution of God's earth. Paul's understanding of God's distributive justice includes divinely mandated economic justice and also more, and it is that "more" that we emphasize here. God's distributive justice means that God is equally available to all—that God's Spirit is distributed freely to each and every one of us to transform God's world into a place of that same justice. Distributive justice is the very nature, essence, and character of God. Or, to use language from our earlier chapters, the distributive justice of God at the center of Paul's gospel and in this letter means that a Spirit transplant is available to all, both Jews and Gentiles.

Finally, to relate the distributive justice of God to the title of this chapter, justification by grace through faith, we emphasize that the Greek word translated "justice" or "righteousness" (as justice) is also the root of the words translated "justification" and "justified." Justification by grace through faith, about which we will soon say more, means God's way of making us and the world just.

We return to Paul's thesis statement: the gospel is "the power of God for salvation" (recall that "salvation" for Paul and the Bible generally is primarily about *this* life, not about *after* this life; about this world, not about "heaven" after death). And it is available "to the Jew first and also to the Greek."

Where Paul uses "Greek" in Romans and Galatians we use "Gentile." Both terms mean "non-Jews," but with a definite adversarial edge. They refer much less to, say, the Celts or the Chinese than to the great imperial nations (Latin *gentes*) the Jews knew all too well from past subjection or present oppression. They could all be summarized as "Greek" because it was the military-backed cultural imperialism of Alexander the Great that had presented the greatest threat to Jewish tradition and identity from the fourth century BCE onward. But now, of course, although the Greek sword was long gone, the Roman sword was still sheathed in a Greek scabbard.

THE JEW FIRST BUT ALSO THE GREEK

God's passion, says Paul, is to forge a unity from "the Jew first and also the Greek" (1:16; 2:9–10). But right now, prior to this future divine unity, there exists an unfortunate unifying feature on the human level. Paul accuses humanity of universal failure, since "all, both Jews and Greeks, are under the power of sin," so that, between them, "there is no distinction, since all have sinned and fall short of the glory of God" (3:9; 3:22–23). The unity of Jews and Greeks, that is, of all the world, is already there, as it were, but it is a unity under sin.

To establish his cosmic criticism Paul, reversing his opening sequence, looks at the Greeks first in 1:16–2:16 (please read) and then at his fellow Jews in 2:17–3:18 (please read). His basic premise is that there is *a common divine law for all humanity*, with one version written in the promises and traditions of the Jews and the other version unwritten but in the hearts and conscience of the Gentiles. But it is the same God, known to Jews from the covenant and to Gentiles from creation.

For both Greeks and Jews, however, "it is not the hearers of the law who are righteous in God's sight, but the doers of the law who will be justified" (2:13). That sentence, by the way, is a good place to see that "righteous" and "just" (or "righteousness" and "justice") mean exactly the same thing for the Bible at large and Paul in particular. Never interpret "righteous(ness)" to mean, in our modern sense, an overly showy piety or religiosity that may be sincere, but probably is not. For Paul, to do what is just is to do what is right, and to do what is right is to do what is just—and this holds true for God as well as for us.

First, what, for Paul, is wrong with the Gentiles in 1:16–2:16 (please read along with us)? He cites two failures, and both come straight from standard anti-Gentile synagogue polemics—which were as inaccurate, by the way, as gentile anti-Jewish polemics.

One failure is *idolatry:* "They exchanged the glory of the immortal God for images resembling a mortal human being or birds or four-footed animals or reptiles" (1:23). Next, and derived from idolatry (1:24, 26, 28), comes *immorality*. Paul cites a long list (1:26–31), the first of which is homosexuality: "Their women exchanged natural intercourse for unnatural, and in the same way also the men, giving up natural intercourse with women, were consumed with passion for one another. Men committed shameless acts with men and received in their own persons the due penalty for their error" (1:26–27).

Paul, like other contemporary Jewish moralists, singled out homosexuality as not only bad, but even "unnatural," in that indictment. But, in that tradition as in many others, sexual nature was determined by biology, body, and genitals. For many people today, however, sexual nature is determined by chemistry, brain, and hormones. So Paul never faced the question we must now both face and answer. Yes, of course, sexual action follows sexual nature, but by what and by whom is sexual nature determined? And what if homosexuality is as "natural" for some as heterosexuality is for others? And recall, of course, that Paul—and presumably his contemporaries—found long hair on men and short hair on women "against nature" in 1 Corinthians 11:14–15. We would surely call that a judgment conditioned by time and place, given locally by culture and not universally by nature.

Second, what, for Paul, is wrong with his fellow Jews in 2:17–3:18 (please read along with us)? How do they fit into his indictment of universal human sin? His basic accusation is that they do not live up to their claims or their ideals:

> You, then, that teach others, will you not teach yourself? While you preach against stealing, do you steal? You that forbid adultery, do you commit adultery? You that abhor idols, do you rob temples? You that boast in the law, do you dishonor God by breaking the law? (2:21–23)

That is actually quite a stretch. When Gentiles, for example, reproached Jews, it was not so much for the hypocrisy of their infidelity as for the irrationality of their fidelity to a covenantal law those Gentiles considered superstitious. Furthermore, when Paul says that "a person is a Jew who is one inwardly, and real circumcision is a matter of the heart—it is spiritual and not literal" (2:29), a contemporary Jew like Philo of Alexandria would have responded, "Of course, but you should have both circumcisions, with the inward manifested by the outward."

All in all, 1:16–3:18 is a fairly shallow indictment of universal sinfulness, but rather than dismissing it as superficial we might ponder its deeper accuracy. There seems to be something profoundly wrong and seriously askew, if not with human nature then at least with the normalcy of human civilization, with what Paul and we have also called the "wisdom of this world." It is true, as Paul says, that we have laws and declarations that we do not follow and that thereby bear witness to our insincerity, if not hypocrisy.

Think, for example, of a great nation that pledges "liberty and justice for all," but seems somewhat unmoved by its failure to achieve it. Or, even worse, think about how humanity has, in a horrible evolution, moved from nineteenth-century imperialism through twentieth-century totalitarianism into twenty-first-century terrorism. We are now forced to wonder about the normalcy of civilization itself, and that makes us reread Paul's accusation of global sin today on a deeper level than when he first wrote it. Maybe, of course, he just saw the same global flaw, but expressed it in the only language available to him from his past and present tradition, while we must do the same now in the more radical language of our past and present experience.

THE RIGHTEOUSNESS OF GOD HAS BEEN DISCLOSED

What, then, is the solution to the global failure, cosmic sinfulness, or universal human chasm between the declared ideal and its actual accomplishment? Here is Paul's answer—and his first three foundational terms: the *righteousness* of God is granted for the *justification* of humanity through the *sacrifice* of Christ (3:25–26). Each of those terms has been profoundly misunderstood and has thereby rendered Paul's theology incomprehensible.

Righteousness: distribution, not retribution. Recall, from above, that God's righteousness means exactly the same as God's justice. But, unfortunately, for us, justice has come to mean primarily *retributive* justice, that is, punishment. Not, however, for Paul—and that is where we start to misunderstand him. For Paul, first, God's justice is *distributive* rather than retributive; second, distributive justice is the very nature, essence, and character of God; and, third, divine distributive justice is above all else God's very being as distributed freely to us to transform God's world into a place of that same justice.

If, however, you misread Paul as announcing that God is a God of retributive justice, you will need theological contortions to explain how that could possibly be "good news" (gospel), especially for that universal human sinfulness described in Romans 1–3. Paul's actual good news, however, is that God's own character of distributive justice is available for anyone willing to accept it—without prior merits or conditions.

Justification: transformation, not imputation. If you misread the justice of Paul's God as retributive, the only good news might be that God would pretend, as it were, that we were just, that God would impute to us a justice we did not have. Such an "as if" treatment would have horrified Paul. There is nothing, for example, about fictional imputation of justice, but everything about factual transformation by justice in these claims from 2 Corinthians:

> All of us, with unveiled faces, seeing the glory of the Lord
> as though reflected in a mirror, are being transformed

into the same image from one degree of glory to another; for this comes from the Lord, the Spirit. (3:18)

We do not lose heart. Even though our outer nature is
wasting away, our inner nature is being renewed day by
day. (4:16)

If anyone is in Christ, there is a new creation: everything old
has passed away; see, everything has become new! (5:17).

That is transformation, not imputation.

Sacrifice: participation, not substitution. We saw in Chapter 5 that
Paul's understanding of sacrificial atonement must be emphatically distinguished from Anselm's interpretation of it as *substitutionary* sacrificial atonement. Indeed, Paul's own interpretation
of Christ's execution was as a *participatory* sacrificial atonement.
That is why, in Romans, having mentioned "Christ Jesus whom
God put forward as a sacrifice of atonement by his blood" in just
one verse (3:25), Paul does not develop that further, yet spends a
whole chapter on our *participation in Christ* (6:1–23).

Humanity's universal sin is far, far worse than those traditional vice lists cited for Greeks and Jews by Paul in Romans
1–3. It is this: we have accepted violence as civilization's drug of
choice, and our addiction now threatens creation itself. Christ's
life was the incarnate revelation of a nonviolent God, and it was
consummated by his death from the violent injustice he had
opposed justly and nonviolently. His death was a sacrifice, was
something "made sacred," as we saw above, because it was the
ultimate witness to the character of his God and the ultimate
invitation for us to participate with him. And we participate by
dying—metaphorically and really—to civilization's violent normalcy or by dying—literally and really (unfortunately often still
necessary)—from the same dominational evil we oppose.

JUSTIFIED BY GOD'S GRACE AS A GIFT

Grace as free gift. We are now "justified by God's grace as a gift" (3.24). What does that mean? In Romans, Paul's Greek word *charis* is usually translated "grace" and understood to mean a free gift. He speaks about being "justified by his grace as a gift" (3:24), about "the free gift in the grace of one man, Jesus Christ" (5:15), and, like a drumbeat, about "the free gift . . . the grace of God and the free gift . . . the free gift . . . the free gift . . . the abundance of grace and the free gift of righteousness" (5:15–17). But be very careful here. There is no such thing as a free gift. There can only be a free *offer*, which becomes a free *gift* when it is accepted.

As a physical analogy, think about the air we breathe. It is always and equally available for everyone in any normal place or time. We do nothing to obtain it, nothing to merit it, and it is there unconditionally for good people and bad people alike. On the one hand, it is absolutely transcendent, since we depend on it totally. On the other, it is absolutely immanent, since it is everywhere inside and outside us, all around us. Indeed, we hardly notice the air unless something goes wrong with us or with it.

Air, however, is a *free offer* that only becomes a *free gift* when we accept it and cooperate with it. We are always free either to take in too little air and choke or to take too much and hyperventilate. Furthermore, if we choose asphyxiation or hyperventilation, we should not say that the air is punishing us. It is always a matter of collaboration and participation with what is already there everywhere.

Paul's good news (gospel) is that God's righteousness—that is, God's very character as distributive justice—is a grace, a free gift offered to us all absolutely and unconditionally for our justification—that is, for our collaboration with God in the transformation of God's world. In other words, God's primary distribution is of God's own self, own nature, own being, own character, or, as Paul prefers to say, God's own Spirit. It is from that primary distributive justice, which is God's gift of self, that the secondary distributive justice, which transforms the world, must come.

Faith as total commitment. As any free offer must be activated into a free gift by free acceptance, so must the gift of God's self, the grace of God's universal offer of a Spirit transplant, be accepted by faith. To continue our analogy: believing is to grace as breathing is to air. And, as always, watch for misunderstanding. *Faith* does not mean theoretical assent to a proposition, but *vital commitment to a program.* Obviously, one could summarize a program in a proposition and believe in that proposition, but faith can never be reduced to factual assent rather than total dedication. Faith (Greek *pistis*) is a total life-style commitment.

Furthermore, faith as commitment is always an interactive process, a bilateral covenant that presumes faithfulness from both parties with, of course, all appropriate differences and distinctions. As Paul emphasizes in Romans, therefore, God and Christ are faithful to the world and so, in faith response, is the world meant to be faithful to them. God's righteousness in Christ is faithfully consistent, and Christians should be consistently faithful in response to that gift of grace.

Abraham is Paul's great model for that response of faith as total commitment to God's gift of self. Abraham was, says Paul, the common ancestor of Gentiles, who live by faith *without* circumcision, as well as of Jews, who live by faith *with* circumcision. "Or is God the God of Jews only? Is he not the God of Gentiles also? Yes, of Gentiles also" (3:29).

Works as unfair polemic. With "works" we have two major chances for misunderstanding. When Paul contrasts faith and works, it is his shorthand for faith-with-works versus works-without-faith and should always be seen as such. Here again an everyday analogy may help us with a correct interpretation of his theology.

An immigrant family opens a restaurant in this country, works very hard, prospers magnificently, and acquires full citizenship. In gratitude, loyalty, and patriotism, they hoist the American flag above their business every morning. Patriotism-with-flag is faith-with-works. But down the block another family with a restaurant decides it better get a flag as well in case it loses business to the newcomers. Flag-without-patriotism is works-without-faith. That is a very valid distinction and an ever present possibility in politics or religion.

But it also generates a major problem. If you drove down that block, how would you tell one restaurant with a flag from the other? How can you tell which is which from viewing the restaurant or even from listening to the owner? You could judge both to be faith-with-works, both works-without-faith, or one the former, the other the latter. You can see how easily cheap polemics and mean accusations can arise in controversies and conflicts.

Personal example. We write books and receive royalties from them. On amazon.com some reviewers who dislike our theology suggest we write only to make money. Our books are not faith-with-works, but works-without-faith. But how can one absolutely prove or disprove such an accusation? Whenever, therefore, you read an accusation of works-without-faith—yes, even from Paul—be careful to assess how much is accurate description and how much is unanswerable polemic. And this is unfinished business to which we return in the next major section on the unity of Jews and Christians.

APART FROM THE LAW SIN LIES DEAD

Works and law. Notice, to begin with, that Paul's Greek says: "apart from law sin lies dead" (7.8)—it is not "the Law" or Torah of Israel but all "law." Once again, watch out for misunderstanding.

Paul not only contrasts *faith* as his shorthand for *faith-with-works* to *works* as his shorthand for *works-without-faith*, he also contrasts faith to law and very often combines them as faith versus works of the law. He does it once in Galatians 2:16: "We know that a person is justified not by the works of the law but through faith in Jesus Christ." And he repeats it again in Romans 3:28: "We hold that a person is justified by faith apart from works prescribed by the law."

On the one hand, any non-Christian Jewish theologian would have responded: "Of course, Paul, we know that. We are justified by the grace of our covenantal relationship with God of which the law is the external sign, public manifestation, and visible commitment." On the other hand, Paul can speak positively of "the law of Christ" in Galatians 6:2, "the law of faith" in Romans 3:27, and "the law of the Spirit of life in Christ Jesus" in Romans 8:2. He also says, "The whole law is summed up in a single commandment, 'You shall love your neighbor as yourself'" in Galatians 5:14 and, twice, "love is the fulfilling of the law" in Romans 13:8–10. Is Jewish "law" bad, but Christian "law" good? Or, from our contemporary point of view, if life under law is so good for political life, how can it be so bad for religious life?

Put bluntly, what is wrong with law as far as Paul is concerned? Is there something more profoundly wrong with law than the ordinary danger of faith-with-works-of-the-law becoming works-of-the-law-without-faith (that is, in our analogy, of patriotism-with-flag becoming flag-without-patriotism)?

There are two interactive problems with law for Paul. One is that its presence establishes knowledge and responsibility for obedience. We admit by its very statement that we know what we should do. The other is that legal articulation does not bring with it any internal empowerment toward accomplishment. An example is the 55-mile-per-hour speed limit posted on our highways; it establishes what we should do, but does not empower us unerringly to do it.

Law and sin. By "law" Paul means *all law,* not just Jewish law, but Roman law; not just human law, but divine law; not just the written law of covenant, but the unwritten law of conscience. So what is wrong with all law and even divine law for Paul? Here is his specific criticism: "The law brings wrath; but where there is no law, neither is there violation" (4:15); "Apart from the law sin lies dead" (7:8).

Does Paul mean that murder, for example, only arises from, because of, or in reaction to the law against it? Does he mean that law provokes sin, command provokes disobedience? Not at all. It is simply that law establishes knowledge, asserts that we now know this or that is wrong, this or that should not be done. If, for example, people declare that all have equal and inalienable rights, they already know that this situation should prevail, they have admitted that they know this, and, unless thereafter they follow through, their very own law condemns them. That 55-mile-an-hour sign does not provoke you unerringly to drive at 75, but it does establish that you now know going over 55 is wrong. You cannot disobey a nonexistent law.

Law gives the power of knowledge (we should not do this), but it does not bring inherently with it the power of obedience (we will not do this). "I do not understand my own actions," says Paul in the name of law, "for I do not do what I want, but I do the very thing I hate" (7:15). This is not a personal or individual confession of inadequacy by Paul before Jewish Torah, but a structural or systemic confession by humanity before its best laws and most sincere ideals. It is the chasm between knowledge and will or conscience and action.

Law, declares Paul, establishes information, but not transformation. Law informs conscience externally, declares Paul, but faith empowers it internally. Remember Philemon and Onesimus from Chapter 2? Will Philemon liberate Onesimus freely and willingly from his heart, motivated by his committed Christian faith? Or will he liberate Onesimus because he feels forced to do so simply to appease Paul or even to obey Christian law? Will he act by faith or by works of Christian law?

Sin and death. Paul says, "Just as sin came into the world through one man, and death came through sin, and so death spread to all because all have sinned" (5:12). That summarizes his earlier assertion that that "all die in Adam," that "the last enemy to be destroyed is death," and that "the sting of death is sin, and the power of sin is the law" (1 Cor. 15:22, 26, 56). That is certainly clear, but is it right?

First, in preindustrial society about one-third of those surviving birth were dead by six, two-thirds by sixteen, and three-quarters by twenty-six years of age. In the ancient world and in all those places where the modern world is still ancient, death is not life's future and distant end, but its present and constant companion. Even apart from death by the famine and plague of war, there was death from disease, malnutrition, and exhaustion caused by injustice.

Christ's "death" always meant for Paul the terrible death of an unjust execution, the horrible death of a shameful crucifixion. It did not mean death as the normal end of life. His theology was not built on Christ's death and resurrection as if Christ had died at home in Nazareth and rose there on the third day. Christ's death was the result of injustice and violence. Here, then, after two thousand years and especially as the twentieth-first century's terrorism replaces the twentieth century's totalitarianism, we ask this question. Is it death or is it violence that is the last enemy of God? Or, better, is it unjust and violent death that is the last enemy of God?

THE GROANING OF CREATION

Paul's vision in Roman 1–8 concerns the unity of Greeks and Jews, that is, of all people, in a transformed world of global peace. But the vision of imperial Rome was also about the unity of all people in a transformed world of global peace. The confrontation is not, therefore, about ends, but about means. Is that final consummation to come as peace through violent victory and pacification or as peace through nonviolent justice and justification?

We ourselves might not consider the distinction between Gentiles and Jews *the* or even *a* major division of the global family. We might think of the haves and the have-nots, of the First World and the Third World, of those who have more than they need and those who can barely survive. But, in any case, it is and always will be about the world. So Paul concludes this section with a magnificent hymn not just to our freedom but to that of creation itself:

> For the creation waits with eager longing for the revealing of the children of God; for the creation was subjected to futility, not of its own will but by the will of the one who subjected it, in hope that the creation itself will be set free from its bondage to decay and will obtain the freedom of the glory of the children of God. We know that the whole creation has been groaning in labor pains until now; and not only the creation, but we ourselves, who have the first fruits of the Spirit, groan inwardly while we wait for adoption, the redemption of our bodies. (Rom. 8:19–23)

Paul mentions "creation" five times in those five verses. Hear, then, the voices of God and Bible, Jesus and Paul as they whisper insistently against the chorus of our narcissistic individualism: "It's about the world, dummy. It's about the world."

THE UNITY OF JEWS AND CHRISTIANS

Paul moves next to a narrower division within that world separated into Gentiles and Jews. He focuses on the division within Judaism between non-Christian Jews and Christian Jews, between Jews who have not accepted Jesus as their Messiah and those who have.

Paul had originally hoped that a unified community of non-Christian Jews and Christian Jews would be the future of Judaism. God would create that unity "not from the Jews only but also from the Gentiles" (9:24) so that "there is no distinction between Jew and Greek; the same Lord is Lord of all and is generous to all who call on him" (10:12). But by the mid-50s when he wrote to the Romans, he already knew that something had gone seriously wrong with that expected unity. It was not happening and already looked like it would not happen. Hence this stricken cry: "I have great sorrow and unceasing anguish in my heart. For I could wish that I myself were accursed and cut off from Christ for the sake of my own people, my kindred according to the flesh" (9:2–3). For Paul, however, this was not just a human problem to be solved, but a divine "mystery" (11:25) to be pondered. So his first focus is on God and how or why God has permitted this to occur.

Divine purpose. Paul searches his Jewish scriptures for precedents and finds many examples of God's unexpected choices and surprising reversals. Isaac, Abraham's son by Sarah, was chosen by God over Ishmael, his older son by Hagar (9:7–9). Then, after Isaac married Rebecca, their younger son, Jacob, was chosen by God over their older son, Esau (9:10–13). That, says Paul, is God as Divine Potter, who can "make out of the same lump one object for special use and another for ordinary use" (9:19–21). Paul then continues his biblical survey by citing those prophets who had long ago announced that God would choose a "people" from among the pagans (9:24–26), but only a "remnant" from among the Jews (9:27–29).

What, then, about the great majority of Jews who have not accepted Jesus as their expected Messiah? Even as Paul faces what is for him a devastating reality, he never says that "even those of Israel" (11:23) are lost, condemned, and abandoned by God. Instead, we get a second emotionally charged cry: "I ask, then, has God rejected his people? By no means! I myself am an Israelite, a descendant of Abraham, a member of the tribe of Benjamin. God has not rejected his people whom he foreknew" (11:1–2). So what is God's purpose in all of this?

Paul's eschatological vision of God's great cleanup of the world was for Jews and Gentiles to combine into one ultimate community in the sequence "the Jew first and also the Greek" (1:16; 2:9–10). But God, says Paul, has reversed that process. Now it is first the Gentiles and only then the Jews who receive the message: "So I ask, have they stumbled so as to fall? By no means! But through their stumbling salvation has come to the Gentiles, so as to make Israel jealous" (11:11). In other words, "a hardening has come upon part of Israel, until the full number of the Gentiles has come in" (11:25).

What is most striking in this whole section is the solemn warning to "you Gentiles" with which Paul concludes his entire exposition (11:13–36). He warns them sternly and lengthily, for example, against boasting and self-confidence with a striking image of Israel as an ancient and domesticated olive tree into which they are but wild and newly grafted branches (11:17–24). He emphasizes that all of this is a divine "mystery" (11:25), but today, after two thousand years, we can and must speak even more fully than Paul ever could.

He said to the Gentiles, "As regards the gospel they [non-Christian Jews] are enemies of God for your sake; but as regards election they are beloved, for the sake of their ancestors; for the gifts and the calling of God are irrevocable" (11:28–29). We now say what Paul never imagined. *There are two covenants, one Jewish and one Christian, both free gifts of divine grace, both accepted initially and lived fully by faith.* That is the only way, *today,* to reread what Paul called God's "mystery" in the face of continuing history.

Human problem. Paul's emphasis on the (non)unity of Jews and Christians as a divine mystery in 9:1–29 and 11:1–36 deliberately frames his discussion of it as a human problem in 9:30–10:21. We are back once again with that problem of faith (with works) versus works (without faith). Is Paul accusing all non-Christian Jews of externalism, of expecting righteousness and justification to derive simply from fulfilling legal requirements? If he were, it would be simply crude polemics; any opposing theologian would have told him, as seen already, that righteousness and justification come from the grace of an internal covenantal relationship and the law is its necessary external manifestation. So should the section in 9:30–10:21 be dismissed as simple polemics? No, because it is time to recall—and probably reread—the sections on those gentile "God-worshipers" from Chapter 3.

We saw there that Paul eventually and successfully focused his Damascus mandate from God and Christ on gentile "God-worshipers," those non-Jewish sympathizers who attended the synagogue and were located religiously between full Jews and pure Gentiles. For many Jews this was a deliberate missionary strategy, a quite adequate way of turning those individuals away from idolatry and immorality without the requirements of full conversion (for example, male circumcision), to which there was some amount of familial and social opposition.

But Paul could never accept that as a missionary strategy. He saw gentile "God-worshipers" as lost between worlds, because they were following some Jewish legal requirements while not accepting the full Jewish faith. Paul could never imagine a half-Jewish, half-gentile person. Was that not, precisely, a classic example of works-without-faith? He warned the Romans, on another subject, for example, about those who "do not act from faith" by asserting that "whatever does not proceed from faith is sin" (14:23).

In other words, by attending the Jewish synagogue, gentile God-worshipers admit that something there is profoundly correct and that they should convert to Judaism. By not doing so, therefore, they are in "sin" and what they are doing is works (without faith) rather than faith (with works). What is happening is not a struggle between Paul and his fellow Jews over Christ *for them,* but over Christ *for the God-worshipers.* It is a struggle between, on the one hand, Paul's Christian missionary strategy and, on the other, Jewish synagogue missionary strategy, for the hearts and minds of those gentile sympathizers. Paul accuses them—and all Jews who support them—of attempting righteousness (justification) by law, by works, and by works of the law.

Paul has a valid case, but not an infallible one. At the end of the fourth century as Christianity became the religion of the Roman Empire, a Jew might have responded like this: "Now do you see the problem? Gentiles have swamped you, they have swallowed you. You think you have converted them, but they have converted you. If you are as good as you think you are, just be yourself and let mission by attraction succeed where mission by conversion may fail." Or, as Paul concludes: "O the depth of the riches and wisdom and knowledge of God! How unsearchable are his judgments and how inscrutable his ways. . . . For from him and through him and to him are all things. To him be the glory forever" (11:33, 36).

THE UNITY OF JEWISH CHRISTIANS
AND GENTILE CHRISTIANS

We turn finally to the concluding chapters of Romans, but leave aside these three sections: 12:14–13:10 and 16:1–16, seen already in Chapters 4 and 2, respectively, and 15:22–33, to be seen in our Epilogue. We focus here on the innermost circle of Paul's narrowing focus on unity, on that between Jewish Christians and gentile Christians within the several Roman assemblies (12:1–15:21).

Recall that, as Paul writes this letter, Claudius has just died in 54 CE and the teenaged Nero has become the new emperor. It was a moment, as we saw earlier, when the poet Calpurnius Siculus could tell his Romans: "Amid untroubled peace, the Golden Age springs to a second birth . . . while he, a very God, shall rule the nations" (*Eclogue* 1.42, 46). It was also a moment when Paul could tell his Romans: "Do not be conformed to this world, but be transformed by the renewing of your minds" (12:2), but still, "If it is possible, so far as it depends on you, live peaceably with all" (12:18). That would be, under Nero, a very big "if," indeed.

What strikes you immediately about 12:1–15:21 is Paul's admonitions not only to external peace, but especially to internal peace. "Live in harmony with one another," he says in 12:16 and 15:5. Furthermore, Paul advises the Roman communities "not to think of yourself more highly than you ought to think, but to think with sober judgment, each according to the measure of faith that God has assigned" in 12:3. Later, he tells them, "The faith that you have, have as your own conviction before God" in 14:22. Harmony is required, it would seem, because God has granted them divergences *within* Christian faith or differences *of* Christian faith. What, then, was the exact situation inside and outside Roman Christianity that required such a long plea for peaceful unity?

The weak and the strong. There were clearly two opposing viewpoints within those Roman Christian assemblies, and Paul attempts to bring their proponents together into one overall community for worship. What was causing the two groups not to "welcome one another" (15:7)?

Paul—somewhat tendentiously—calls one group the "weak" and the other group the "strong." The "weak" are those for whom Jewish observance of kosher dietary laws and the religious calendar was still important. These could, of course, be either Christian Jews or Christian God-worshipers. The "strong" are those for whom such observance was unnecessary. "Some believe in eating anything, while the weak eat only vegetables. . . . Some judge one day to be better than another, while others judge all days to be alike" (14:2, 5).

With regard to theory and his own position, Paul is quite clear: "I know and am persuaded in the Lord Jesus that nothing is unclean in itself; but it is unclean for anyone who thinks it unclean" (14:14). He puts himself, therefore, among the "strong," who do not consider Jewish observances necessary for either Christian Jews, Christian God-worshipers, or Christian Gentiles. "*We* who are strong." he says in 15:1, "ought to put up with the failings of the weak, and not to please ourselves."

With regard to practice and the groups' own situation, Paul is equally clear. Speaking to both, he says, "Those who eat must not despise those who abstain, and those who abstain must not pass judgment on those who eat; for God has welcomed them" (14:3). The common basis for unity even in that disagreement is this:

> Let all be fully convinced in their own minds. Those who observe the day, observe it in honor of the Lord. Also those who eat, eat in honor of the Lord, since they

> give thanks to God; while those who abstain, abstain in
> honor of the Lord and give thanks to God. (14:5–6)

Therefore, he insists, the weak should not "pass judgment" on the strong, nor the strong "despise" the weak (14:4, 10, 13).

While speaking to the weak, Paul never asks, advises, or commands them to abandon their kosher and calendar observances. Indeed, all he ever says to them is not "to pass judgment" on the strong (14:3, 4, 10, 13).

Paul spends the most time speaking to the strong. He tells them repeatedly and emphatically, "If your brother or sister is being injured by what you eat, you are no longer walking in love. Do not let what you eat cause the ruin of one for whom Christ died" (14:15; also read 14:20–21; 15:1). If, in other words, kosher and calendar observances are not important for you, then neither is their negation. If all food is good, then so is kosher food. If every day is good, then so is the Sabbath. The strong ones are to adjust, get over it, grow up, "for the kingdom of God is not food and drink but righteousness and peace and joy in the Holy Spirit" (14:17). Paul asks each group to accept the other's religious differences, so that they can worship together and share the Lord's Supper (15:6–7). But he also insists that both observance and non-observance must proceed from faith and not from, say, discrimination, contempt, or judgment (read 14:22–23).

From Antioch to Rome. Recall, from Chapter 3, that bitter dispute between Paul, on the one side, and James, Peter, and "even Barnabas," on the other (Gal. 2:1–14). At the end of the 40s CE, Paul, as we saw there, argued—and lost—against them all at Antioch over exactly that same subject as here in Rome. Was the eucharistic meal for a mixed community of Christian Jews and Christian Gentiles to be kosher for all or kosher for none?

The earlier decision there was kosher for none, but James of Jerusalem, brother of Jesus, demanded that it be changed to kosher for all. All the leaders agreed except Paul, who even called Peter a "hypocrite" for reversing his position. For Paul this was solved by a no-concession policy that resulted in his separation from the others and "even Barnabas" (Gal. 2:11–14). We suggested in Chapter 3 that Paul's absolute refusal to compromise on that subject was less theologically than polemically motivated and that that would explain his different response to the exact same meal problem at Rome (Rom. 14).

Here in Romans 14 we get a far better vision of Paul operating from his own theological basis than in that earlier dispute at Antioch. And it has some rather obvious lessons for us today. Those tensions between "weak" and "strong" Christians over Jewish observances within Christianity may sound distantly irrelevant to us after two thousand years of separate identities. But, in that time and place, they were *a* major issue, maybe even *the* major issue. What contemporary intra-Christian disputes will seem just as dated and irrelevant to later Christian centuries as those at Antioch and Rome may seem to us today? But, in any case, how Paul sought to resolve those ancient disputes may still be paradigmatic for later intra-Christian disagreements. In any such debates, the "strong" are those who "despise" the "weak," while the "weak" are those who "judge" the "strong," and to both Paul says, "Welcome one another, just as Christ has welcomed you, for the glory of God" (15:7) and "not for the purpose of quarreling over opinions" (14:1).

WITH FEAR AND TREMBLING

In his letter to the Romans the good news (gospel) from Paul is that the divine self, the Spirit of God, is freely offered to all—without prior merits or conditions—but that we humans are still free to accept or decline it. In summary, the distributive justice of God is our justification coming as grace to be accepted by faith. With that understanding of his theology, we had one very special question for Paul.

We wanted to know why he tells the Philippians, "Work out your own salvation with fear and trembling" (2:12b). In fact, Paul is even more emphatic in the original Greek than in the English translation: "With fear and trembling, work out your salvation." Why does he put fear and trembling first and make God a God of terror?

We decided it would be wise to read the entire sentence, to read the phrase in context. Paul tells the Philippians:

> Work out your own salvation with fear and trembling;
>   for it is God who is at work in you,
> enabling you both to will and to work for his good
> pleasure. (2:12b–13)

True, there is a lot more there than fear and trembling, but the question persisted. If God is doing all the willing and the working, why are we doing all the fearing and the trembling? If it all depends on us, we can see how we might be punished for our failure, but if God is doing everything in us and for us, why should there be any need for trembling fear?

To begin with, Paul mentions "work" three times in that single sentence, once at the start, once in the middle, and once at the end. This seems to put an end once and for all to any discussion of whether there can be faith-without-works, the internal commitment without the external manifestation. There cannot be. The problem, as seen already, is not that there can be faith-without-works, but that there can be works-without-faith. You cannot have love without show, but you can always have show without love.

In an effort to understand how God actually works within us to empower both intention and operation, we return to that earlier example from medical technology. In a heart transplant, a person's old and damaged heart is totally removed and replaced by a new and undamaged one. It is possible that the new organ may be rejected by the body, but there are medications to help prevent this.

What God did in Christ and what God thereby offers to everyone is an identity change, a character replacement, a Spirit transplant. God's own holy Spirit, the Spirit of nonviolent distributive justice that is God's own self, nature, and character, is offered freely and gratuitously to all people. It is what Paul calls a *charis* and we translate as a "grace." It is a free gift offered without any prior conditions demanded by God or prior merits expected of us. Indeed, how could either of those even be imagined? Also, to continue the analogy, the medications against the rejection of God's Spirit transplant are called prayer and meditation, worship and liturgy.

Paul calls that process of Spirit transplant "God's just-making" or "God's just-ification" of the world. But what is truly extraordinary is not so much that the divine Spirit transplant is freely offered by God, but that it is freely offered to friends and enemies alike—yes, even to God's enemies—according to Jesus: "For God makes his sun rise on the evil and on the good, and sends rain on the righteous and on the unrighteous" (Matt. 5:45).

That absolute grace—offered even to God's enemies—is what Paul could never forget, because he experienced it personally at Damascus. It was precisely when he was, as he told the Philippians, a "persecutor of the church" that God empowered him to live in Christ (3:6). It was precisely when he was, as he told the Galatians, "violently persecuting the church of God and . . . trying to destroy it" that God's Spirit transplant took place within him (1:13). It was precisely "while we were God's enemies," as he told the Romans, that "we were reconciled to God through the death of his Son" (5:10).

That Spirit transplant, though freely offered to God's friends and enemies alike, never destroys the human freedom also given us by that same God. We are always free to accept it or reject it. Acceptance is what Paul calls "faith" and, of course, that does not simply mean belief in the free offer, an abstract and theoretical acknowledgment that this free offer is available. "Faith" means a grateful submission to the Spirit transplant of God's own nonviolent distributive justice, which empowers us to will and enables us to work toward a reclamation of this world in collaboration with God.

Finally, however, there is still that question of working out our salvation with fear and trembling. We can only conclude that the reason we should fear and tremble about our salvation is not because God will punish us if we fail, but because the world will punish us if we succeed.

❈

CHAPTER SEVEN

LIFE TOGETHER "IN CHRIST"

ALTHOUGH CONVERSION is a personal process, Paul did not simply convert individuals. Paul created communities. He converted people to a new life in community, to life together "in Christ." The phrase is shorthand for a way of life in community radically different from that in the normal societies of this world.

We treated "in Christ" briefly in Chapter 5 in the context of Paul's understanding of Christ crucified and at-one-ment. There we spoke of becoming one with Christ, in Christ, by being crucified with him, dying and rising with him, participating in his death and resurrection. In that sense, "in Christ" is a metaphor for a new personal identity and orientation toward life—the kind of life that results from a "Spirit transplant."

But life "in Christ" for Paul was not primarily about a new personal identity for individuals. Paul's understanding was very different from a widespread understanding of the role of "religion" and the purpose of "spirituality" in modern Western culture, where they are often thought of as primarily private, individual matters, even though many Christians would say that being Christian also means being part of a church. For Paul, life "in Christ" was *always* a communal matter. This was so not simply because "it's important to be part of a church," but because his purpose, his passion, was to create communities whose life together embodied an alternative to the normalcy of the "wisdom of this world."

"IN CHRIST," "SPIRIT OF CHRIST," "BODY OF CHRIST"

In this chapter, we focus on the communal meaning of life "in Christ." Our purpose is to see what Paul's communities looked like "on the ground." We begin with Paul's ways of speaking of the new community. "In Christ," the title of this chapter, is shorthand for Paul's vision of Christian community. The phrase, one of his favorites, appears over a hundred times in the letters of the radical Paul, often with a communal meaning.

Paul had other favorite phrases for Christian life together. To be "in Christ" was also to be "in the Spirit." He uses these phrases interchangeably. In a single chapter in Romans, he writes, "There is therefore now no condemnation for those who are *in Christ Jesus*" (8:1). In the very next verse, he refers to *the Spirit of life in Christ Jesus* (8:2). A few verses later: "You are *in the Spirit, since the Spirit of God dwells in you*. Anyone who does not have *the Spirit of Christ* does not belong to him" (8:9). After a few more verses, he speaks of *the Spirit of God* (8:14). Paul's communities "in Christ" were communities "in the Spirit," grounded in the Spirit of God as known in Jesus.

Paul speaks not only of the "Spirit of Christ," but also the "body of Christ." This metaphor dominates most of 1 Corinthians 12, where Paul combines Spirit language with body language:

"For *in the one Spirit* we were all baptized *into one body*—Jews or Greeks, slaves or free—and we were all made *to drink of one Spirit*" (12:13). Near the end of the chapter, Paul puts it in a sentence: "You are the *body* of Christ" (12:27). Christian communities were the "*body* of Christ" animated by the "*Spirit* of Christ." Their identity and their life together "in the body" were grounded in Christ, in the Spirit, in the Spirit of God as known in Christ, and not in "this world."

We add one more image—implicit this time in a single word, not a phrase. Paul regularly addressed his communities as "brothers" ("brothers and sisters," in the inclusive language of recent translations of the New Testament). The term appears more than fifty times in his genuine letters. To address people as brothers (and sisters) was not just social convention. Nor was it just about affection, though affection was of course involved.

It was more—it was "new family" language, describing what social historians sometimes call a "fictive family" to distinguish it from a biological family. The use of new family language implies that members of the community have the same obligations to each other as biological brothers and sisters do. In the urban world of Paul, where extended biological families had been broken apart, diminished, and sometimes lost completely because of migration to the cities and high death rates, these communities were "new families" in which members had the same responsibility to care for each other that biological families did. These were to be communities of caring and sharing.

All of these images had their home in Paul's conviction that the "new age" had begun. The term "new age" in our time is sometimes associated with "New Age" movements that are negatively regarded by many Christians. But the language is biblical and eschatological.

Paul was convinced that the *eschaton,* God's dream for the world, had begun in Christ and that it was a process already under way. God's great cleanup of the world had begun, and his communities were part of the "new creation," of the way the world is meant to be. "If anyone is in Christ, there is *a new creation:* everything old has passed away; see, everything has become new!" (2 Cor. 5:17). He also uses the language of "new creation" in the midst of a conflict that we shall soon look at more closely: "For neither circumcision nor uncircumcision is anything; *but a new creation is everything!*" (Gal. 6:15). "New creation" language is not just about new individuals, but about a new world, a new era, a new age. This, for Paul, was what life "in Christ," "in the Spirit," "in the body of Christ" was about.

SHARE COMMUNITIES

We presume, though Paul never says so, that his communities "in Christ" were what we call "share communities." By this we mean communities in which there was a sharing of material as well as spiritual resources.

We do not imagine that this involved what the book of Acts says about at least one of the earliest Christian communities in Jerusalem:

> All who believed were together and had all things in common; they would sell their possessions and goods and distribute the proceeds to all, as any had need. (2:44–45)

We leave that aside for now, but will return to it in more detail in this book's Epilogue.

From Paul's letters, it is clear that his converts did not sell all that they had and give the proceeds to the community. There were people in his communities who were better off financially than others. And yet there are compelling reasons for imagining that his communities were "share communities."

The first is grounded in what we know about Jesus. Bread—meaning the material basis of existence—mattered greatly to him. His message was about the kingdom of God, highlighted among other places in the Lord's Prayer. Immediately after the petition for the coming of God's kingdom *on earth* is a prayer for bread: "Give us this day our daily bread." God's kingdom—Paul's life "in Christ"—includes bread. Bread—the material basis of life—was central to Jesus's passion. There is no reason to think that Paul dropped this emphasis.

A second reason is the economic fragility of ordinary people in the urban environment of Paul's activity. Their income came from work and ranged from a bit more than what was adequate for subsistence through an adequate amount to a less than adequate amount. Few would have had any significant savings. This meant extraordinary vulnerability to loss of work, whether through illness or accident or a drop in demand for their labor or skill. We imagine that the people in Paul's communities took care of each other: if some couldn't work or find work for a period of time, those who had enough would share with them. The language of "new family" implies as much: members of his communities had the same obligations to each other as did members of a biological family.

Third, there is indirect but persuasive evidence that Paul's communities were share communities in two post-Pauline letters (that is, letters attributed to Paul, but not among the seven letters of the radical Paul). In both cases, the issue is "freeloaders," a problem that often occurs in share communities. Some people are attracted to such communities because it's a good deal—they will be taken care of. This is the context for a text from 2 Thessalonians:

> When we were with you, we gave you this command:
> Anyone unwilling to work should not eat. For we hear

that some of you are living in idleness, mere busybodies,
not doing any work. Now such persons we command
and exhort in the Lord Jesus Christ to do their work quietly and to earn their own living. (4:10–12)

This text has sometimes been quoted by Christians to justify
a conservative economic policy: those who do not work should
not be taken care of. But it is not a heartless command that
anybody who does not work, regardless of the reasons, should
starve. Rather, the text reflects that in these share communities
some were abusing the practice. It means, in short, that if you
can work and you're not willing to, perhaps not even trying to
look for work, then you are not to receive the benefits of the
share community. The need for such a command demonstrates
that these were in fact share communities.

The problem of "freeloaders" is also treated in 1 Timothy 5:3–
16, written in Paul's name around or soon after the beginning of
the second century. The issue is the financial support of widows,
which tells us that the community was supporting widows. The
passage begins, "Honor widows who are really widows." As it
continues, it names several criteria for discerning who is a real
widow, urges families who can take care of their widowed members to do so, and ends with, "Let the church not be burdened
[with caring for widows who aren't real widows] *so that it can
assist those who are real widows.*" As in the previous passage from
2 Thessalonians, this counsel would not have been necessary if
the community were not a share community.

We turn now to case studies of texts that illustrate central
qualities of life "in Christ" as a "new creation." As briefly mentioned, Paul did not in his letters describe what life in these communities was to be like. Nevertheless, because his letters often
addressed issues and conflicts that had arisen in his absence, his

responses give us glimpses of what he thought life "in Christ" embodied.

CHRISTIAN JEWS AND CHRISTIAN GENTILES IN GALATIA

Our first case study focuses on the best-known verse from Paul's letter to the Galatians: "There is no longer Jew or Greek [Gentile], there is no longer slave or free, there is no longer male and female; for all of you are one *in Christ* Jesus" (3:28). We already saw the importance of this verse in Chapter 4. But, although it is very familiar, its full weight and radical meaning can be seen only be contextualizing it within Galatians and the conflict in Galatia as a whole.

Paul's community in Galatia was in Asia Minor, probably in ancient Ancyra, Ankara in modern Turkey. Paul had established a community there apparently without planning to do so—he mentions that it was only because of a physical affliction that he stopped there: "You know that it was because of a physical infirmity that I first announced the gospel to you" (4:13). The Galatians had received him with great hospitality:

> Though my condition put you to the test, you did not scorn me or despise me, but welcomed me as an angel of God, as Christ Jesus. . . . For I testify that, had it been possible, you would have torn out your eyes and given them to me. (4:14–15)

As we said in Chapter 3, we can only guess at the nature of this affliction, but our best scholarly conjecture is that Paul suffered from chronic malaria.

But during his absence, things changed. The central issue was circumcision. Did male gentile converts need to be circumcised in order to be in the community "in Christ"? Some were being persuaded that the answer was yes. We do not know precisely who Paul's opponents were. But if those gentile converts were former God-worshipers, we can easily imagine them being pulled in two different directions—toward traditional Judaism by the synagogue and toward Christian Judaism by Paul.

We do know that the opposition to Paul in Galatia was fierce. We know from the letter that his opponents challenged his authority and impugned his credentials as an apostle. They also appealed to the authority of sacred scripture, the Jewish Bible, which was also Paul's Bible. Indeed, they had the Bible on their side. In Genesis, God's covenant with Abraham emphatically required circumcision: "This is my covenant, which you shall keep, between me and you and your offspring after you: Every male among you shall be circumcised" (17:10). Circumcision is mentioned another five times in the next four verses in Genesis. So it had been for males entering the Jewish covenant with God ever since. Who was Paul to set aside the clear command of the Bible? Especially since he was proclaiming a Jewish Messiah?

The fierceness of the conflict is pointed to by the fierceness of Paul's response. Galatians is the most polemical of his letters—and for Paul, that's saying a lot. It is his only letter that does not begin with a thanksgiving. Instead, he immediately counters his opponents attack upon his authority: "Paul an apostle—sent neither by human commission nor from human authorities, but through Jesus Christ and God the Father, who raised him from the dead" (1:1). Then indignation, accusation, and condemnation pour out:

> *I am astonished* that you are so quickly deserting the one who called you in the grace of Christ and are turning to a different gospel—not that there is another gospel, but there are some who are confusing you and *want to*

pervert the gospel of Christ. But even if we or an angel from heaven should proclaim to you a gospel contrary to what we proclaimed to you, *let that one be accursed!* As we have said before, so now I repeat, if anyone proclaims to you a gospel contrary to what you have received, *let that one be accursed!* (1:6–9)

Soon thereafter he calls them "foolish Galatians" and wonders if they have become possessed: "You foolish Galatians! Who has bewitched you?" (3:1).

Near the end of the letter, his passion surfaces again:

> *Listen! I, Paul,* am telling you that if you let yourselves be circumcised, *Christ will be of no benefit to you.* . . . I am confident about you in the Lord that you will not think otherwise. But *whoever it is that is confusing you will pay the penalty.* (5:2, 10)

He concludes the section with sarcasm (whose etymology is "a gashing of flesh"): "I wish those who unsettle you would *castrate* themselves!" (5:12).

Why this passion about circumcision? Because requiring circumcision for gentile male converts countered Paul's most foundational sense of his mission as well as his vision of what "in Christ" meant. His vocation was to be an apostle to the Gentiles—and for him that did not mean first converting Gentiles to Jews through circumcision so that they could then be baptized into Christ. For him to have accepted that notion would have meant a betrayal of his calling. And it would have countered his vision of what life "in Christ" in "the new creation" was like.

Paul's counterarguments (note the plural) are not really addressed to his opponents. We assume he was aware that he didn't have much chance of changing their minds. Rather, he sought to persuade those in the community who were wavering, uncertain about what to think. He begins his defense of his apostleship by reminding them of his Damascus experience and call (1:11–24). He continues by reporting that Christian leaders in Jerusalem had approved his mission to the Gentiles ("the uncircumcised") *without* requiring that they be circumcised (2:1–10).

Then he turns to the strongest point of his opponents' argument: the biblical text requiring circumcision of Abraham and his offspring. He mounts a number of counterarguments, only some of which we mention. He appeals to another text about Abraham from a few chapters earlier in Genesis, before the text requiring circumcision. "Abraham 'believed God, and it was reckoned to him as righteousness'" (Gal. 3:6, quoting Gen. 15:6). Paul also uses this argument in Romans 4:9–10, where he explicitly adds that faith was reckoned to Abraham as righteousness *before* he was circumcised.

Then he continues: "So, you see, those who *believe* are the descendants of Abraham. . . . Those who *believe* are blessed with Abraham who *believed*" (Gal. 3:7, 9). Believing—faith—is what makes a person a descendant of Abraham, not circumcision. We hasten to add that believing and faith are not about a set of beliefs, but a relationship of commitment and trust. Paul's point about Abraham is central also to his contrast between justification by "works of the law" versus "through faith in Jesus Christ," treated more fully in our previous chapter on Romans.

We note in passing a rather curious argument that Paul makes about Abraham. He writes that, according to Genesis:

> God's promises were made to Abraham and to his offspring; it does not say, 'And to offsprings,' as of many; but it says, 'And to your offspring,' that is, to one person, who is Christ. (3:16)

Paul treats the plural noun "offspring" ["seed" in earlier translations] as if it were a singular noun. We don't know if Paul thought this would be persuasive, or if he (and his hearers?) smiled at this. In any case, his point was clear: the promise to Abraham carried forward to a singular descendant and thus referred to Christ—and so those who are "in Christ" are heirs to the promise, apart from circumcision.

Paul also appeals to the Galatians' own experience. Right after addressing them as "foolish" and "bewitched," he reminds them: "It was before your eyes that Jesus Christ was publicly exhibited as crucified" (3:1). Obviously, he did not mean that they were at the crucifixion; he refers to the message he had taught while with them. Then he asks:

> The only thing I want to learn from you is this: Did you receive the Spirit by doing the works of the law or by believing what you heard? Are you so foolish? Having started with the Spirit, are you now ending with the flesh? Did you experience so much for nothing?—if it really was for nothing. Well then, does God supply you with the Spirit and work miracles among you by your doing the works of the law, or by your believing what you heard? (3:2–5)

Paul reminds them that they had experienced the Spirit—the Spirit of God, the Spirit of Christ—prior to their emerging preoccupation with the question of circumcision. They had experienced a Spirit transplant without circumcision—why now the concern with the flesh, with circumcision?

All of this is the context for the passage about being "one in Christ," which we now quote in full (you will recall it from Chapter 4):

> In Christ Jesus you are all children of God through faith. As many of you as were baptized *into Christ* have clothed yourself *with Christ.* There is no longer Jew or Greek

[Gentile], there is no longer slave or free, there is no longer male and female; for all of you are one *in Christ* Jesus. And if you belong *to Christ,* then you are Abraham's offspring, heirs according to the promise. (3:26–29)

Note that Paul is not making a universal statement about humankind. That is, he is not simply saying "we are all one." Rather, his claim is that "in Christ" there is no longer Jew or Gentile, slave or free, male and female. That is, in the "new creation," already under way, in the new age "in Christ," these divisions are gone. We note also the juxtaposition of this passage with Paul's asking the Galatians to remember how they experienced the Spirit. Communities "in Christ" live by the Spirit of Christ—they are those who have undergone a Spirit transplant. Once again, life "in Christ" and life centered in the Spirit (of God/Christ) go together.

We turn now to a concluding important and crucial question. Was Paul's emphasis about being one "in Christ" about unity or equality? The two are not the same. In a time of national crisis, an American president might say, "We are all Americans." The message would be clear: despite our differences, we are united in our concern and love for our country. But it would not mean we are all equal. So, is Paul's message about being "one in Christ" about unity rather than division? Or about equality rather than superiority and hierarchy?

We are persuaded that Paul's response to the conflict in Galatia is about equality and not simply unity. We don't think he was saying, "Can't we all just get along, despite our differences?" That might be a good thing, and would be better than much of what we have had since. But Paul's vision was about more than this. It was about equality instead of acceptance of hierarchy and superiority within Christian community. In Chapter 2, we argued that in Paul's letter to Philemon, his vision of life "in Christ" meant that a Christian master could not have a Christian slave. We also argued that men and women were to be equals in the community. So also here. The issue is equality between Christian Jew and Christian Gentile, even though uncircumcised. Equality, not simply unity, is the hallmark of the new creation.

RICH AND POOR IN CORINTH

Corinth was the only city in which Paul's communities contained significant class divisions between the wealthy and powerful and ordinary people. The division is named early in the letter: "Not many of you were wise by human standards, not many were powerful, not many were of noble birth" (1 Cor. 1:26). To say "not many" also indicates *that some were.*

If we ask how the Christian community in Corinth came to include some who were wealthy and powerful, the answer probably lies in architecture, specifically the architectural relationship between urban villas and shops, whether workshops or retail shops. Urban villas were often located on major streets in cities, and their ground floors facing the street were commonly rented out as shops. This created the possibility of contact between aristocratic families living in a villa and people working in shops connected to the villa, like Paul and his co-workers Priscilla and Aquila and others (see, for example, Acts 18:2–3, 18–19; 1 Cor. 16:19). This had happened in Corinth. And aristocratic families took for granted the hierarchical social arrangements that marked the normalcy of that world.

The presence of some wealthy and powerful people among Christians in Corinth is the context for many of the issues addressed in Paul's letters to Corinth. These include, for example, Paul's emphasis on "Christ crucified" as the subversion of the normalcy of that world, which we treated in Chapter 5; taking financial disputes into civil courts (6:1–8); marriage between a stepson and a widowed stepmother to protect patrimony (5:1–13); and attending celebratory dinners in pagan temples and buying and eating meat that came from animals sacrificed at such gatherings (10:14–33). These were problems for the haves rather than the have-nots.

This is the setting in which Paul addresses an issue about the way the Lord's Supper was observed at Corinth (11:17–34). In Paul's communities (and generally among early Christians), the Lord's Supper was a real meal, a "share meal," and not simply a ritual involving a morsel of bread and a sip of wine. From what Paul says in this chapter, the Lord's Supper began with the breaking of the bread, which was followed by the meal, and concluded with the passing of the cup *after* the meal (11:24–25; note "after supper" in v. 25). The meal was framed by bread and wine in remembrance of the final meal of Jesus.

But this was not what was happening at Corinth. Paul's comments in this section of Corinthians presume that the meal was being hosted by those in the community who were wealthy and powerful, most likely in a villa. At the beginning of the section on the Lord's Supper, Paul writes:

> I do not commend you, because when you come together it is not for the better but for the worse. For, to begin with, when you come together as a church, I hear that there are divisions among you. . . . When you come together, it is not really to eat the Lord's Supper. (11:17–18, 20)

Why this judgment? Why is what they are doing "not really" the Lord's Supper? Paul continues:

> Each of you goes ahead with your own supper, and one goes hungry and another becomes drunk. What! Do

you not have homes to eat and drink in? Or do you show contempt for the church of God and humiliate those who have nothing? (11:21–22)

The issue here is that not everybody got to eat the same food. The wealthy had their own food and drink, and others had little or nothing. This practice was common in the Roman world when a wealthy patron hosted a meal that included people from lower social classes. The patron would serve finer food and wine to others from his social rank and less fine food and wine to those of lower rank. Meals, even when they crossed social boundaries, would nevertheless mirror those boundaries.

Paul's counsel near the end of the section suggests an additional problem: "So then, my brothers and sisters, when you come together to eat, *wait for one another*" (11:33). The implication is clear: some arrived early and began to eat and drink at once. Who would arrive early? Not those who had to work for a living, but those who had leisure—that is, the wealthy and powerful. And so eating together a shared meal framed by the breaking of the bread and the passing of the cup was not happening.

Thus the way the Lord's Supper was practiced at Corinth reflected the social hierarchy and inequality of that world. This is what Paul protests against, and this is the context for his warning:

Whoever, therefore, eats the bread or drinks the cup of the Lord in an unworthy manner will be answerable for the body and blood of the Lord. Examine yourselves, and only then eat of the bread and drink of the cup. For all who eat and drink without *discerning the body*, eat and drink judgment against themselves. (11:27–29)

In some Christian denominations, the words about partaking "in an unworthy manner" have been understood to mean in an unworthy state of repentance, and "without discerning the body" as referring to failing to discern the real presence of Christ in the bread and wine. But in Paul's context, something simpler and at the same time more important is meant: "discerning the body" refers to the *community* as the body of Christ. The way the Lord's Supper was being practiced at Corinth denied the equality of life "in Christ," life in the body and Spirit of Christ. Instead, it perpetuated the gulf between rich and poor and conformed life "in Christ" to the normalcy of this world.

Instead, "in Christ" everybody is to be at the same table and eat the same meal. Don't literalize this—it's not about monotony of food, though it precludes monopoly of food. Within the community, everybody is equal and should get the same—it is a share meal, a sharing of God's stuff, of God's earth. Everybody gets enough. This is the supper of the Lord.

HIERARCHY AND SPIRITUAL GIFTS IN CORINTH

The community in Corinth was divided not only by hierarchy and inequality based on material wealth and power. Some were also claiming superiority based on the possession of particular spiritual gifts. The issue was speaking in tongues, or glossolalia, to use the technical term. Some saw glossolalia as a public manifestation of having received the Spirit of God, the Spirit of Christ, and therefore as evidence of spiritual superiority. The problem and Paul's response take up the next three chapters of his first letter to Corinth, 12–14.

We begin by noting that speaking in tongues in Corinth was not the same phenomenon as reported in the story of Pentecost in Acts 2:4–11. There, speaking in tongues resulted in universally understandable language. "Filled with the Holy Spirit," the followers of Jesus spoke, and people "from every nation," who spoke many different languages, all understood what they were saying:

> Amazed and astonished, they asked, "Are not all these who are speaking Galileans? And how is it that we hear, each of us, in our own native language? . . . In our own languages we hear them speaking about God's deeds of power." (Acts 2:7, 11)

Everybody understood what was being said, even though they did not know the language in which it was said. This emphasis on universally intelligible language reverses the story of the Tower of Babel, in which the people of the earth were scattered into different nations and languages (Gen. 11). The coming of the Spirit at Pentecost was the beginning of the undoing of Babel.

But in Corinth, speaking in tongues was an unintelligible form of ecstatic speech. It involved an ecstatic state of consciousness during which unintelligible sounds came forth. It was a "private" language, not a universal language as in Acts.

Paul's response was twofold. On the one hand, there should be no hierarchy of persons based on spiritual gifts. Specific gifts—and glossolalia in particular—did not mean that some people were spiritually superior to others. Rather, there are varieties of spiritual gifts and they all come from the same Spirit:

> Now there are varieties of gifts, but the same Spirit; and there are varieties of services, but the same Lord; and there are varieties of activities, but it is the same God who activates all of them in everyone. To each is given the manifestation of the Spirit for the common good. (12:4–7)

The "varieties of gifts" included some that were ecstatic and some that were not: wisdom, knowledge, faith, healing, miracles, prophecy, discernment of spirits, tongues, and the interpretation of tongues (12:8–10). All, he emphasizes again, "are activated by one and the same Spirit" (12:11).

Paul then moves from "Spirit of Christ" language to "body of Christ" language. Just as all the parts of a body are necessary and meant to serve each other, so it is within the body of Christ: "For just as the body is one and has many members, and all the members of the body, though many, are one body, so it is with Christ" (12:12). All the parts of the body matter. No part of the body should lord it over another part (12:14–26). In Christ, people are equal—everybody matters.

Yet, on the other hand, there is a hierarchy of the gifts themselves, even though not a hierarchy of persons based on those gifts. The gift of prophecy is more important than speaking in tongues (14:2–25). This does not dismiss glossolalia; it is one of the gifts and, far from dismissing it, Paul says, "I thank God that I speak in tongues more than all of you" (14:18). But it is neither evidence of spiritual superiority nor the greatest gift.

Rather, the greatest spiritual gift is love. In the middle of this three-chapter treatment of the gifts of the Spirit is the best-known text from Paul, 1 Corinthians 13. Often read at weddings and funerals, it may even be the most famous chapter in the New Testament as a whole. Its fame is deserved, for it is gorgeous, lyrical, and luminous.

The last verse of chapter 12 sets it up: "Strive for the greater gifts. And I will show you a still more excellent way" (12:31). Chapter 13 begins with a series of contrasts as Paul extols the supreme importance of love:

> If I speak in the tongues of mortals and of angels, but do not have love, I am a noisy gong or a clanging cymbal. And if I have prophetic powers, and understand all mysteries and all knowledge, and if I have all faith, so as

to move mountains, but do not have love, I am nothing. If I give away all my possessions, and if I hand over my body so that I may boast, but do not have love, I gain nothing. (13:1–3)

Then he lists the qualities of love:

Love is patient; love is kind; love is not envious or boastful or arrogant or rude. It does not insist on its own way; it is not irritable or resentful; it does not rejoice in wrongdoing, but rejoices in the truth. It bears all things, believes all things, hopes all things, endures all things. (13:4–7)

He again proclaims the priority of love as a spiritual gift over the gifts of prophecy, tongues, and knowledge:

Love never ends. But as for prophecies, they will come to an end; as for tongues, they will cease; as for knowledge, it will come to an end. For we know only in part, and we prophesy only in part; but when the complete comes, the partial will come to an end. (13:8–10)

Then he contrasts childish and adult ways of knowing:

When I was a child, I spoke like a child, I thought like a child. I reasoned like a child; when I became an adult, I put an end to childish ways. (13:11)

Yet there are limits to our knowing. We know only in part, even though we are already fully known by God:

For now we see in a mirror, dimly, but then we will see face to face. Now I know only in part; then I will know fully, even as I have been fully known. (13:12)

This famous chapter then climaxes with its most famous verse:

> And now faith, hope, and love abide, these three; and the
> greatest of these is love. (13:13)

There is a hierarchy of spiritual gifts, and the most important gift is love. The context of 1 Corinthians 12–14 gives this text an even richer meaning than when it is heard, as it most often is, apart from that context.

First, the love of which Paul speaks is a spiritual gift, not simply an act of will, not something we decide to do, not simply good advice for couples and others. Rather, as a spiritual gift, love is the most important result (and evidence) of a Spirit transplant. As the primary fruit of the Spirit, it is also the criterion by which the other gifts are evaluated.

Second, when this text is heard apart from its context, it often sentimentalizes, trivializes, and individualizes what Paul meant by love. It should not be reduced to a tribute in praise of love. Nor should its meaning be reduced to being nice, sensitive, thoughtful, faithful, and kind, even though those are fine qualities. And it should not be reduced to behavior in individual relationships, important as that is.

Rather, for Paul, love in this text is radical shorthand for what life "in Christ" is like—life in the "new creation," life "in the Spirit," life animated by a Spirit transplant. As the primary fruit of a Spirit-filled life, love is about more than our relationships with individuals. For Paul, it had (for want of a better word) a *social* meaning as well. The social form of love for Paul was distributive justice and nonviolence, bread and peace. Paul's vision of life "in Christ," life in the "new creation," did not mean, "Accept the imperial way of life with its oppression and violence, but practice love in your personal relationships."

To make the same point differently, people like Jesus and Paul were not executed for saying, "Love one another." They were killed because their understanding of love meant more than being compassionate toward individuals, although it did include that. It also meant standing against the domination systems that ruled their world, and collaborating with the Spirit in the creation of a new way of life that stood in contrast to the normalcy of the wisdom of this world. Love and justice go together. Justice without love can be brutal, and love without justice can be banal. Love is the heart of justice, and justice is the social form of love.

TWO WAYS OF LIFE: FLESH AND SPIRIT

Paul's letter to his conflicted community in Galatia provides another description of life "in Christ." As in 1 Corinthians 13, the text emphasizes love as the primary quality of living by the Spirit:

> For you were called to freedom, brothers and sisters; only do not use your freedom as an opportunity for self-indulgence, but *through love become slaves to one another.* For the whole law is summed up in a single commandment, *"You shall love your neighbor as yourself."* . . . *Live by the Spirit,* I say. (5:13–14, 16)

Then, using the language of "flesh" and "Spirit," Paul contrasts two comprehensive ways of life:

> Do not gratify the desires of the flesh. For what the flesh desires is opposed to the Spirit, and what the Spirit desires is opposed to the flesh; for these are opposed to each

> other, to prevent you from doing what you want. . . . Now
> the works of the flesh are obvious: fornication, impurity,
> licentiousness, idolatry, sorcery, enmities, strife, jealousy,
> anger, quarrels, dissensions, factions, envy, drunkenness,
> carousing, and things like these. (5:16–21)

The central contrast between "flesh" and "Spirit" has often been misunderstood. Many who revere Paul as well as many who don't like him have often identified "flesh" with "body," as if our bodies *as flesh* are the primary problem and temptation. Given the common meaning of the word "flesh" in English, this is not surprising. Thus many have seen Paul as anti-body. Some approve; some think this is weird.

This misunderstanding is encouraged by several items in his list of the "works of the flesh": fornication, impurity, licentiousness, drunkenness, and carousing, all of which can be construed as bodily sins, as sins of the flesh. But for Paul, the "works of the flesh" include much more: sorcery, enmities, strife, jealousy, anger, quarrels, dissensions, factions, and envy. These are not evils flowing out of being embodied. As Paul uses the word "flesh," it is not to be identified with our bodies, as if the problem is that we are embodied creatures who eat and drink and have sex.

Rather, the "works of the flesh" are characteristics of a comprehensive way of life that stands in contrast to life in Christ, life in the Spirit. They are the result of being centered in something other than the Spirit of God as known in Jesus. Abstractly, life centered in the flesh is life centered in the finite. More concretely, it is living by the "wisdom of this world," the normalcy of the domination systems of his time. That life is marked by enmities, strife, jealousy, anger, quarrels, dissensions, factions, and envy.

The other way of life, the alternative to life centered in the "flesh," is life centered in the Spirit:

By contrast, the fruit of the Spirit is love, joy, peace, patience, kindness, generosity, faithfulness, gentleness, and self-control. There is no law against such things. And those who belong to Christ Jesus have crucified the flesh with its passions and desires. If we live by the Spirit, let us also be guided by the Spirit. (5:22–25)

It is important not to be distracted by the familiarity of his list of the "fruit of the Spirit." It is a remarkably attractive vision of life, filled with love, joy, peace, patience, generosity, faithfulness, gentleness, and self-control. And this life is the result of a Spirit transplant.

PAUL'S FAREWELL LETTER

We conclude with two texts from Paul's letter to the Philippians. Though it was probably not the last letter he wrote, we call it his farewell letter because Paul imagines that it could be. Paul wrote it from prison, quite possibly during the same imprisonment in Ephesus that produced the letter to Philemon (see Chapter 2). Paul doesn't say why he was in prison, but we know from the letter that it was an imperial prison and that he was aware that his confinement could end in execution (1:12–26).

Philippi in northern Greece was the first city in Europe in which Paul created a community. His relationship with the Philippians seems to have been free of difficulties. No troubles are reported, no pressing questions are addressed; rather, the letter is filled with affection. Because he knew that this might be his final farewell to a community that he loved, his words carry extra weight. The possibility of death has a sobering effect.

Given this, the letter's dominant tone of thanksgiving, joy, and lack of worry is remarkable. We turn to our first text, from near the end of the letter:

Rejoice in the Lord always; again I will say, Rejoice. . . . Do not worry about anything, but in everything by prayer and supplication with thanksgiving let your requests be made known to God. And the peace of God, which surpasses all understanding, will guard your hearts and your minds in Christ Jesus. (4:4, 6–7)

Paul follows this with a concise description of the kind of life he wishes for them—the life of those who are "in Christ." It includes a list of virtues and concludes with a description of the kind of life he himself had found "in Christ":

Finally, beloved, whatever is true, whatever is honorable, whatever is just, whatever is pure, whatever is pleasing, whatever is commendable, if there is any excellence and if there is anything worthy of praise, think about these things. Keep on doing the things that you have learned and received and heard and seen *in me,* and the God of peace will be with you.

I have learned to be content with whatever I have. I know what it is to have little, and I know what it is to have plenty. In any and all circumstances I have learned the secret of being well-fed and of going hungry, of having plenty and of being in need. I can do all things through him [Christ] who strengthens me. (4:8–9, 11–13)

This is who Paul had become because of his life in Christ. It is an enviable state: he had learned to be content with whatever came his way, with being hungry or well fed, with having plenty or being in need, in any and all circumstances. Paul's Spirit transplant had been successful.

The second text from Philippians is perhaps the fullest concise distillation of the theology of the radical Paul. Philippians

2:1–11 speaks of what life "in Christ" is to be like and it empha-sizes "Christ crucified" and "Jesus Christ is Lord." It also contains what most scholars think is a hymn, written by either Paul or a predecessor. We think it probably comes from Paul; but even if it was written by a predecessor, it is evidence for the nature of Paul's thought, for Paul obviously used it approvingly. And whether written by Paul or a predecessor, it is of special interest because it is the earliest Christian hymn we have.

The text begins with a series of counsels about behavior for those who are "in Christ":

> If then there is any encouragement in Christ, any conso-lation from love, any sharing in the Spirit, any compas-sion and sympathy, make my joy complete: be of the same mind, having the same love, being in full accord and of one mind. Do nothing from selfish ambition or conceit, but in humility regard others as better than yourselves. Let each of you look not to your own inter-ests, but to the interests of others. (2:1–4)

The text continues by grounding the mind they are to have—the mind they are to have in Christ—in what they see in Jesus: "Let the same mind be in you that was in Christ Jesus" (2:5). And what mind is that?

Then the text quotes or echoes the hymn—this is the mind that they are to have. We display the hymn in three parts, with-out presuming that they correspond to stanzas:

> *Who, though he was in the form of God,*
> *did not regard equality with God*
> *as something to be exploited,*
> *but emptied himself,*
> *taking the form of a slave,*
> *being born in human likeness.*

And being found in human form,
he humbled himself
and became obedient to the point of death—
even death on a cross.

Therefore God also highly exalted him
and gave him the name
that is above every name,
so that at the name of Jesus
every knee should bend,
in heaven and on earth and under the earth,
and every tongue should confess
that Jesus Christ is Lord,
to the glory of God the Father. (2:6–11)

This is a hymnic summary of the story of Jesus. Of course, there is much in the story of Jesus as we know it from the gospels that is not here. But what is here encapsulates Paul's most central convictions about Jesus.

The second and third parts (stanzas?) emphasize "Christ crucified" and "Jesus Christ is Lord"—which, not coincidentally, are the titles of two of our chapters. Note that in part two, when Paul refers to Jesus becoming "obedient to the point of death," he adds specifically, "even death *on a cross*." For Paul, Jesus didn't just die—he was crucified by the imperial power of his day as an advocate of a vision of life other than imperial normalcy, a vision of life different from the "wisdom of *this* world."

Part three is perhaps the most triumphant proclamation of "Jesus Christ is Lord" in the New Testament. Immediately following the reference to Jesus dying on a cross, the hymn proclaims, "Therefore God also highly exalted him" (as the first fruits of the resurrection) "and gave him the name that is above every name." Then the text refers to the three-story universe of the ancient imagination: "so that at the name of Jesus every knee should bend, in heaven and earth and under the earth." It concludes with language that explicitly countered Roman imperial theology: "and every tongue . . . confess that Jesus Christ is Lord, to the glory of God." Jesus is Lord—the emperor is not. Jesus is Lord—the rulers of this world are not.

Look again at the first part of the hymn and the beginning of the second:

> *Though he [Jesus] was in the form of God,*
> *[he] did not regard equality with God*
> *as something to be exploited,*
> *but emptied himself,*
> *taking the form of a slave,*
> *being born in human likeness.*
> *And being found in human form, he humbled himself . . .*

The passage is filled with contrasts. What we see in Jesus is very different from what we see in someone else, but what is the contrast? Who was it that regarded "equality with God as something to be exploited," or as "something to be grasped at," as another translation puts it? And what was the "emptying" of Jesus about?

This passage is understood in different ways by contemporary scholars. Two possibilities have been suggested most often, to which we add a third. One possibility is that the contrast is with Adam. According to Genesis, the temptation to which Adam and Eve yielded was the desire "to be like God." Thus what we see in Adam (as symbol of all humanity) is a desire to be godlike. Jesus lived another path: he did not seek equality with God. In support of this understanding, we note that Paul elsewhere speaks of the contrast between the "first Adam" (the Adam of Genesis) and the "second Adam" or the "last Adam" (Jesus; Rom. 5:12–14; 1 Cor. 15:45–49). In this interpretation, Adam and Eve's sin was *hubris,* a Greek word commonly translated "pride." Pride as *hubris* does not mean simply feeling good about an achievement, but making oneself the center of existence, puffing oneself (or one's cause) up to inordinate size. This is what the "first Adam" did. The second Adam presents us with a different model—Jesus emptied himself.

A second way of understanding the contrast sees this text as referring to the preexistent Christ, the prebirth Jesus. Or, to use John's language, the text refers to the "Word" that was with God from the beginning and that became incarnate in Jesus (John 1:1–14). For this understanding, the incarnation meant that the preexistent Christ, the Word, emptied itself of its divine qualities in order to become human in Jesus. Becoming human meant becoming vulnerable—even to the point of being executed by the powers that rule this world. This understanding is commonly called "kenotic," from the Greek word *kenosis,* which means "emptying." The Christ who was with God from the beginning emptied himself in order to be among us.

There is a third possibility. Who was it in Paul's world who claimed to be "in the form of God" and who regarded "equality with God as something to be exploited"? The answer is quite obvious: the Roman emperor, who was proclaimed by imperial theology as divine, Lord, Son of God, and the Savior of the World, who had brought peace on earth.

It is not necessary to decide among these interpretations. They might all be present, even as we think the third is the most probable. If the contrast is to Adam and Eve, we need to recall that they were the parents not only of the murdered Abel, but of the murderer Cain, who according to Genesis founded the first city and thus the domination systems that began five or six thousand years ago. If the contrast is to the preexistent Christ, a similar point emerges: God, self-emptied and incarnate in Jesus, was passionate not about power and control, but about justice and peace, distributive justice and nonviolence.

And if the contrast is between Christ and Caesar, the other meanings need not be excluded. All make the same claim. What we see in Jesus—Christ crucified and raised as "Jesus Christ the Lord"—is the way, the path. This, Paul says in this text, is the mind that the followers of Jesus are to have. What we see in Jesus is the way, the path, of personal transformation. And it is the way, the path, of advocacy of a way of life very different from and in opposition to the normalcy of "this world." And it would cost Paul his life.

THE DEATH OF AN APOSTLE

IN THIS EPILOGUE we move into the higher echelons of scholarship known as conjecture. We ask about Paul's death. How, where, and when did he die? All we can offer in reply is educated guesswork, but we will guess as closely as we can to historical probability. We begin with the last words we have from Paul himself.

TO PRESERVE CHRISTIAN UNITY

As we saw in Chapter 2, Paul ended his letter to the Romans by greeting twenty-seven individuals there known to him either by contact or reputation. It is not at all unusual for him to end his letters with farewell greetings, but most are kept very general and individuals are not named. For example: "Greet all the brothers and sisters with a holy kiss" (1 Thess. 5:26), and "Greet one another with a holy kiss" (2 Cor. 13:12).

It is possible that Romans 16 is so different and detailed because Paul is inviting those Christian individuals to assist him as he journeys westward to Spain. But it also possible that he has premonitions that this letter might be, as it actually was, his last will and testament. That shows up at the end of Romans 15 as Paul tells them about his plans to visit them:

> I desire, as I have for many years, to come to you when I
> go to Spain. For I do hope to see you on my journey and
> to be sent on by you, once I have enjoyed your company
> for a little while. . . . I will set out by way of you to Spain;
> and I know that when I come to you, I will come in the
> fullness of the blessing of Christ. (15:23–24, 28–29)

But he continues by noting that, before passing through Rome
to Spain and the west, he has a very special and important mission to accomplish in the east:

> I am going to Jerusalem in a ministry to the saints; for
> Macedonia and Achaia have been pleased to share their
> resources with the poor among the saints at Jerusalem.
> They were pleased to do this, and indeed they owe it
> to them; for if the Gentiles have come to share in their
> spiritual blessings, they ought also to be of service to
> them in material things. (15:25–27)

We return in a moment to consider the content and purpose
of that "ministry to the saints," but as for premonitions, note
how Paul concludes:

> I appeal to you, brothers and sisters, by our Lord Jesus
> Christ and by the love of the Spirit, to join me in earnest
> prayer to God on my behalf, that I may be rescued from
> the unbelievers in Judea, and that my ministry to Jeru-
> salem may be acceptable to the saints, so that by God's
> will I may come to you with joy and be refreshed in your
> company. (15:30–32)

What is this mission to Jerusalem during which, on the one
hand, non-Christian Jews may endanger Paul's life and, on the
other, Christian Jews may negate Paul's ministry? It is another of

those instances where, as in Chapter 3, Luke's Acts must be used to fill out Paul's letters, especially since, after Romans 15–16, we never hear again from Paul himself.

In Chapter 3, we mentioned the Jerusalem conference, at which there was discussion and agreement between James, Peter, Barnabas, and Paul that gentile male converts to Christian Judaism did not need to be circumcised. But it was clearly a bitterly fought discussion, as we saw earlier, from the truculence of Paul's language reporting this incident to the Galatians. He mentions "false believers secretly brought in, who slipped in to spy on the freedom we have in Christ Jesus, so that they might enslave us" (2:4) and "those who were supposed to be acknowledged leaders (what they actually were makes no difference to me; God shows no partiality)" (2:6). You might compare, by the way, the much more irenic, if apologetic, description of that discussion in Acts 15.

But even with that final agreement between James and Peter, on the one side, and Paul and Barnabas, on the other, it was necessary to create, as it were, a sacrament of reconciliation between the Jewish Christian conservative wing and the gentile Christian liberal wing of the earliest church. What was it and how was it to be conducted?

The conservative and ascetic James, known as James the Just, James of Jerusalem, and James the brother of Jesus, led a group in Jerusalem that practiced community life with regard to their possessions, just as Luke tells us in his Acts. In 2:44–45 it is reported that they had "all things in common," and in 4:32–5:11 that "no one claimed private ownership of any possessions, but everything they owned was held in common." They were known, therefore, as the "Poor Ones," because they followed Jesus's injunction, "Blessed are the poor," by practicing a radical divine share life that was counter to the structure of normal human society. And so, after that hard-fought agreement at Jerusalem in which conservatives conceded to liberals, there was to be reciprocal concession whereby liberals donated to the support of James's model community. Or, in Paul's own words, at the end of that Jerusalem conference, "they asked only one thing, that we remember the poor, which was actually what I was eager to do" (Gal. 2:10).

That Jerusalem agreement was that financial donations from Christian Gentiles were to furnish specific support for that utopian eschatological model community of Christian Jews under James in Jerusalem. You will, however, only get the full story of that "collection for the saints" or "contribution for the Poor Ones" by bringing together parts from Paul and parts from Luke:

1. Agreement	Galatians 2:10	
2. Program	1 Corinthians 16:1–4; 2 Corinthians 8–9	Acts 11:27–30
3. Delivery	Romans 15:25–31	Acts 20:4
4. Condition		Acts 21:17–26
5. Disaster		Acts 21:27–36

First, you can see from those texts how much letter space Paul gave to this collection and how great were his care and concern for its accomplishment. Next, you also read above his fears for what might happen to it: James's Christian Jews might refuse it and Jerusalem's non-Christian Jews might attack him. Finally, you can read in Acts that Paul's fears were amply justified. What happened there, according to Luke as our only source?

First, James's community refused to accept the collection *unless* Paul showed that he himself "observed and guarded the law" by using (some of?) the money to pay for a purification ritual in the Temple (Acts 21:24; read 21:17–24). He apparently agreed to accept this admittedly rather ambiguous test.

He was in Jerusalem with a group of Christian Gentiles carrying the collection. Nothing whatsoever prohibited him and those Christian pagan companions from entering the Temple's huge outer Court of the Gentiles, but they would have had to wait for him there while he and the Christian Jews with him passed the warning balustrade and entered the smaller inner courts reserved under penalty of death for Jews alone. Once he had entered the Temple, he was attacked by "Jews from Asia" for violating that ban by bringing those pagan associates into the inner Court of the Jews (Acts 21:27–28). Paul was then arrested and started the long journey to Rome.

Luke, in Acts, does not tell us what eventually happened to Paul when he reached Rome. He never tells us about his death or martyrdom. Once Paul is openly preaching in Rome, the story Luke intended to tell is over. So he simply ends by saying that Paul "lived there two whole years at his own expense and welcomed all who came to him, proclaiming the kingdom of God and teaching about the Lord Jesus Christ with all boldness and without hindrance" (28:30–31). But what happened to Paul after that ending?

THE MARTYRDOM OF PAUL

It is likely that Luke, writing one or two generations after Paul, knew what had happened to him. But he probably did not want to conclude his second volume—Acts—with a Roman condemnation of Paul just as he had finished his first one—the gospel—with a Roman condemnation of Jesus.

In Luke's gospel Pilate had, of course, asserted the innocence of Jesus "a third time" (23:22). And in Acts the viper that left him unharmed "asserted" the innocence of Paul (28:3–6). Still, Luke probably wanted to avoid having both his volumes end with a Roman execution after his repeated claims that Roman authority and pro-Roman Jewish authority considered Christianity to be an innocent phenomenon. So, without either Paul's letters or Luke's Acts to guide us, how and when did that great apostle of Jesus die?

There are two main answers to that question. In both, Paul dies as a martyr under the emperor Nero, but, unfortunately, both operate on the borderline between tradition and scholarship, guess and conjecture, including, of course, our own option for the second one below.

Paul was freed and went to Spain. One general reconstruction proposes that Paul was freed after those "two whole years" mentioned in Acts 28:30, continued on as planned from Rome to Spain, and wrote those six letters judged in this book as post-Pauline and, indeed, anti-Pauline. He eventually returned to Rome and was martyred by Nero. This is based on the account in *1 Clement,* a Christian letter written from Rome to the still contentious Corinthians at the end of the first century. It warns them that "through jealousy and envy the greatest and most righteous pillars of the Church were persecuted and contended unto death" (5:2). So, it continues, "let us set before our eyes the good" (5:3) apostles, first the martyred Peter (5:4) and then the martyred Paul:

> Through jealousy and strife, Paul showed the way to the prize of endurance; seven times he was in bonds, he was exiled, he was stoned, he was a herald both in the East and in the West, he gained the noble fame of his faith, he taught righteousness [Greek *dikaiosune,* or "justification," as in the letter to the Romans] to all the world,

and when he had reached the limits of the West he gave his testimony [*martyrēsas*, or "was martyred"] before the rulers, and thus passed from the world and was taken up into the Holy Place—the greatest example of endurance. (5:5–7)

That text certainly knows the tradition that "Petrus et Paulus," the twin founders of Christian Rome, had replaced "Romulus et Remus," the twin founders of pagan Rome. But those unspecified mentions of "the West" in *1 Clement* 5 are probably based more on Paul's plans for "Spain" in Romans 15:24, 28 than on separate and independent information.

Furthermore, if Luke knew that Paul had been released after Acts 28:30, it is hard to imagine why he would not at least have mentioned it—without necessarily going on to mention his eventual martyrdom. As stated above, every high Roman or pro-Roman authority who confronted Paul in Luke's Acts declared him innocent: the governor Gallio at Corinth (18:14–15); the tribune Claudius Lysias at Jerusalem (23:29); and the governor Festus at Caesarea Maritima (25:18, 25; 26:31).

Had Paul been acquitted, freed, and gone westward to Spain, Luke could surely have added one or two more sentences to that effect. Since every Roman official who met Paul declared him innocent, Luke could scarcely have omitted a climactic imperial judgment of innocence.

Paul was not freed and never went to Spain. Soon after mid-July of 64 CE a terrible fire broke out at the west end of the Circus Maximus and blazed eastward along the valley between the northern Palatine and southern Aventine hills. Of Rome's fourteen regions, three were totally destroyed, seven were severely damaged, and only four were left unharmed, before the fire was finally stopped after a week of urban terror. Tacitus's *Annals*, written in the second decade of the second century CE, tells of the immediate belief that Nero himself ordered the fire:

> Therefore, to scotch the rumor, Nero substituted as culprits, and punished with the utmost refinements of cruelty a class of men, loathed for their vices, whom the crowd styled Christians. . . . First, then, the confessed members of the sect were arrested; next, on their disclosures vast numbers were convicted, not so much on the count of arson as for hatred of the human race. And derision accompanied their end; they were covered with wild beasts' skins and torn to death by dogs; or they were fastened on crosses, and, when daylight failed, were burned to serve as lamps by night. (15.44.2, 4)

Our best historical guess, then, is that Paul, and presumably Peter as well, died among those many Christians martyred by Nero in 64 CE. Paul's death was not the special event of a Roman citizen executed by a privileged beheading, although, of course, that is why Christian iconography usually displays him holding a sword. We suggest that Paul died among all those other Christians rounded up in Nero's scapegoat persecution. If that is correct, he died horribly, but he did not die alone, separate, special, or supremely important.

In the terror of Nero's accusation and the horror of his vengeance, few Christians were able to concentrate on what happened to Paul, Peter, or anyone else. His death is hidden among all those deaths described above in the *Annals* of Tacitus. It is possible that the author of *1 Clement* knew of that inclusion, although, as seen above, he presumed that Paul had reached Spain before his martyrdom. In any case, immediately after mentioning the execution of Peter and Paul, that letter continues by saying, "To these men with their holy lives was gathered a great multitude of the chosen, who were the victims of jealousy and offered among us the fairest example in their endurance under many indignities and tortures" (6:1). Notice, by the way, that Tacitus speaks above of "vast numbers" and *1 Clement* speaks here of "a great multitude . . . among us," referring, we suggest, to that same scapegoat persecution by Nero in 64 CE.

There is a first irony here. Recall the fierce disagreement between Paul and Peter at Antioch in Galatians 2:11–13 from Chapter 3 earlier. They were finally reconciled, at least by later tradition, as martyrs under Nero. Also, recall the disagreement between the "weak" and the "strong" from Romans 14, mentioned in Chapter 6. We do not know if Paul's plea for their unity was successful or not. But, once again, that discord was rendered moot by Nero's brutality. Peter and Paul, "weak" Christians and "strong" Christians, united in martyrdom, were finally able to, as Paul prayed in Romans 15:6, "together with one voice glorify the God and Father of our Lord Jesus Christ."

There is also a second irony. Paul did not know for sure that the letter to the Romans would be his last will and testament. He did know that accompanying the collection to Jerusalem was personally very dangerous. But the letter and the collection were both about unity and, eventually, that search for unity would cost him his life. He accepted that possibility.

That is worth pondering for a moment. It was not Paul himself, but representatives from the assemblies involved who carried the collection to Jerusalem. Paul could, in other words, have refrained from going with them and, instead, gone straight on to Rome and Spain. But that east-to-west axis, the letter to the Romans, and the collection itself were about holding together a Christian unity of conservatives and liberals. It is hard for us today to feel profoundly about that ancient cleavage between Christian conservatives (kosher for all) and Christian liberals (kosher for none). And no doubt future Christianity will find our contemporary dispute between Christian conservatives and Christian liberals equally irrelevant in the long term. Still, there have always been martyrs willing to die for one side or the other. But there have usually been very few who, like Paul, gave their lives in an attempt to hold both together in Christian unity.

Finally, then, we give the last word to Paul himself, speaking about what was ultimately to be that fatal great collection for James's utopian community at Jerusalem. "I do not mean that there should be relief for others and pressure on you," he says in 2 Corinthians 8:13–14,

> but it is a question of a fair balance
> between your present abundance and their need,
> so that their abundance may be for your need,
> in order that there may be a fair balance.

We cite that text as applying not just to the original situation of Paul's collection, but to the present situation of our modern world. It is, then, now, and always, about "a fair balance," or a distributive justice, in which God's family all get an equitable share of God's world.

NOTES

Chapter One
Paul: Appealing or Appalling?

1. Adolf Gustav Deissman, trans. William E. Wilson, *Paul: A Study in Social and Religious History* (New York: Harper & Row [Harper Torchbooks], 1957), pp. 80, 140.

Chapter Three
The Life of a Long-Distance Apostle

1. William Mitchell Ramsay, *The Cities of St. Paul* (New York: Hodder & Stoughton [Doran], 1907), p. 235.

2. William Mitchell Ramsay, *St. Paul the Traveler and the Roman Citizen* (London: Hodder & Stoughton, 1895), p. 60.

3. Ramsay, *St. Paul the Traveler and the Roman Citizen*, p. 61.

4. Rodney Stark, *The Rise of Christianity* (San Francisco: HarperSanFrancisco, 1997), pp. 147–62.

5. Stark, *Rise of Christianity*, p. 160.

INDEX OF SCRIPTURES